SOVIET COMBAT AIRCRAFT

SOVIET COMBAT AIRCRAFT

The Four Postwar Generations

Roy Braybrook

OSPREY
AEROSPACE

Published in 1991 by Osprey Publishing Limited
59 Grosvenor Street, London W1X 9DA

British Library Cataloguing in Publication Data

© Braybrook, Roy
  Soviet combat aircraft.
   1. Soviet Union. Military aircraft 1945 to present
   I. Title
  623.74'6'0989

ISBN 185532120 3

Editor Dennis Baldry
Design Simon Bell
Phototypeset by Keyspools Limited, Golborne, Lancs.
Printed in Great Britain by BAS Printers Limited, Over Wallop, Hampshire

Contents

Preface   8

CHAPTER ONE
Overview   10

CHAPTER TWO
The Subsonic/Transonic Generation   29

CHAPTER THREE
The First Supersonic Generation   66

CHAPTER FOUR
The Less-Long Airfield Generation   103

CHAPTER FIVE
The New Generation   153

Abbreviations   202

Index   206

Preface

My initiation as an aviation writer took place in 1963, when one of my colleagues at Hawker Aircraft, that very accomplished aerospace historian Francis K Mason, left the company to become editor of *RAF Flying Review*. Shortly afterwards he asked me to write a design analysis of the MiG-21 for that journal. At the time I was a project engineer, working for Hawker on the preliminary design of future combat aircraft, and the MiG-21 was one of the potential adversaries on which I was keeping an eye. As a small, single-engined high performance aircraft it was basically a Hawker kind of aeroplane, though somewhat on the light side. It was also a particularly interesting design to discuss, since contemporary aviation magazines had completely misjudged it, imagining from early photos that it followed the trend to high weights established by America's early Century-series fighters.

However, in April 1963 deliveries of the MiG-21 had begun to Finland, and it was photographed with ground crew standing alongside the front fuselage. It was thus a straightforward job to calculate the size of the intake, and thus the mass flow of the engine, and the thrust it could provide. One could also deduce, though with less accuracy, the overall dimensions of the aircraft, and estimate its weight. Analysing the MiG-21 was the type of job that my colleagues and I performed every day of the week, not only on Soviet aircraft, but on French and American products as well.

The resulting article was well received, and led to a series of commissions to produce design analyses of other Soviet combat aircraft. Looking back, the success of the series may have derived in part from credible weight and performance estimates, and partly from the fact that one tried to get the reader to see these fighters and bombers through the eyes of a designer. However, success depended very heavily on some excellent photographs taken by an unnamed photographer during the airshow at Moscow's Tushino airfield in 1961. The story went around at the time (and I have never had any reason to doubt it) that photography on the airfield was forbidden, although military attaches, journalists and a variety of agents took pictures with small cameras that could easily be concealed. In the case of this particular photographer, who had taken along his full professional kit, he never got inside the airfield, because his car 'happened' to break down where the road passed the end of the main runway. He consequently came away with an excellent set of pictures, far better than anything available to Western intelligence from their own sources.

These photographs were offered for publication in the UK, but MoD objected on the grounds that they were so good that their appearance in a magazine would result in an end to Soviet airshows. They were subsequently published in a US journal, and MoD's prediction proved essentially correct. The only subsequent show of any significance was the July 1967 event at Domodedovo, when several variable-sweep and jet-lift projects were shown for the first time. However, this proved to be a one-off event. The Soviets decided not to give away any further information on their combat aircraft, and the shutters came down.

For practical purposes there was then a 21-year gap until the MiG-29 made its public debut at Farnborough in 1988, followed by the appearance of an impressive range of Soviet combat aircraft at Le Bourget in June 1989, and even more at the combined Tushino/Frunze airshow and static display two months later.

The recent outpourings of Soviet information make this an unusually good time to survey developments in the combat aircraft field. However, it is also worth at this stage reconsidering earlier Soviet combat aircraft, if only to place these new types in better perspective. Soviet fighters and bombers from the 1950s and '60s also remain relevant in the sense that current Chinese combat aircraft are mostly variants of older Soviet types. Following the massacre in Peking in June 1989, the West placed on ice many of its technology cooperation programmes relating to China, though it now appears that some of these efforts are being restarted. All current indications are that China's principal combat aircraft will remain derivatives of old MiG projects throughout the 1990s.

Just before the Mikoyan design bureau in Moscow celebrated its 50th anniversary on 8 December 1989, I was contacted by a member of the staff with the suggestion that I should take part in the preparation of an English language version of its official history. I had to decline, since I was already committed to producing this book. The proposal had been made informally, and I dare say that other Western writers were being sounded out at the same time by those concerned with the Mikoyan history. However, the fact that the most famous of all Soviet fighter design bureaus was evidently now willing to open its archives to someone such as myself underlined the vast change that has taken place in Soviet attitudes over the course of a very short period.

Although Mikhail Gorbachev's *glasnost* policy began some years earlier, for students of Soviet combat aircraft the new era really began on 30 August 1988, when two MiG-29s arrived at Farnborough to participate in the airshow the following week. Despite widespread exports of Soviet equipment, and the best efforts of US satellites, we had in reality been deprived of reliable information on Soviet fighters since the Domodedovo show of '67. That gap of 21 years was a very long time in a fast-changing business. One can only trust that this new climate, in which we can see their latest products and talk with their designers and pilots in a very friendly and relatively open way, will continue, and that the post-Gorbachev leadership change will produce no reverse swing in policy that equally suddenly takes Soviet aviation back into the frustrating secrecy of the Cold War.

Roy Braybrook
Ashtead
1991

1 / Overview

SOON it will be 50 years since the beginnings of turbojet-powered combat aircraft development in the Soviet Union. This fact, coupled with the new openness on the part of the Soviets in exhibiting and discussing their military aircraft, make it an appropriate time to review what they have achieved in this field, and where they now stand in regard to fighters, bombers, and fixed- and rotary-wing attack aircraft.

By any standards their progress from the somewhat crude Mikoyan-Gurevich MiG-15 *Fagot* to the world-class Sukhoi Su-27 *Flanker* has been impressive. When swept-wing MiG-15s (referred to by the PLAAF as F-2s) were deployed to Korea in November 1950, despite their thick aerofoils and centrifugal-flow engines their performance came as an unpleasant suprise to American pilots flying piston-engined F-51s and straight-wing F-80C jets. However, in most respects those MiGs were fundamentally inferior to the F-86A-5 Sabres of the 4th Fighter-Interceptor Wing, which were deployed in the following month from Andrews AFB in Maryland.

That imbalance in fighter quality undoubtedly persisted for a long time, but by September 1988, when two MiG-29 *Fulcrums* were presented for the first time at a major Western aerospace show, there was little suggestion of Communist inferiority. Indeed, in some respects the MiG-29 was seen to be better than the best Western aircraft in its class (ie, the F/A-18), and its flying demonstrations of tail-slides and knife-edge passes made it the star of the Farnborough show.

What we did not appreciate at the time was that the MiG-29 was in some respects only the Soviet equivalent of the F-16, ie, a well-established low-classification dual-role aircraft that could be exported virtually anywhere in friendly parts of the world. We discovered at Le Bourget in June 1989 that the Su-27 is a much more important and advanced fighter, their precise equivalent (and in some respects the equal) of the F-15. Whether its radar is as good as the Hughes APG-63 of the F-15 may be doubted, and whether any Soviet air-to-air missile is the equal of the short-range AIM-9M or the medium-range AIM-120 has yet to be established. Nonetheless, judged purely as an airframe-engine combination, the advanced nature of the Su-27 was a startling revelation. Not only did this large fly-by-wire (FBW) aircraft perform tail-slides, but it was also flown (with limiters switched off) in a low level 'Cobra' manoeuvre involving angles of attack (AOA) around 120°, something no existing Western fighter could duplicate.

At Le Bouget the MiG-29 and Su-27 were joined by the Su-25 *Frogfoot* and the rotary-wing Mil Mi-28 *Havoc*. Two months later the MiG-29 appeared at Airshow Canada at Abbotsford, British Columbia, and a CAF Air Command officer (Maj Bob Wade, a CF-18 pilot) was allowed to fly in the two-seater. August also witnessed two major events in the Moscow area: an Aviation Day flypast at Tushino, and a static exhibition at Frunze (also known as Khodynka). The flypast included public debuts by the Beriev A-40 Albatross amphibian (previously known to NATO as Tag-D, after the Tagenrog test centre), the Tupolev Tu-160 *Blackjack* and Tu-26 *Backfire C*, and the Myashichev M-4 *Bison* in the form of the VM-T transporter, with the Energia fuel tank carried piggyback-style. The Frunze line-up included airshow debuts by the MiG-27 *Flogger J*, MiG-25 *Foxbat D*, Su-17 *Fitter*, Su-24MK *Fencer*

D, Yakovlev Yak-38 *Forger A*, Kamov Ka-25 *Hormone*, Ka-29 *Helix B*, Mi-14 *Haze A*, Mi-17 *Hip H*, and the Mi-26 *Halo* in military form. That September both the Mi-28 and the Mi-24 *Hind F* (export designation Mi-35P) were shown at Heli-tech '89 at Redhill in England, and the Ka-29 made its Western debut at Hanover in May 1990. To complete this list of revelations, in February 1990 when the MiG-29 and Su-27 were present at Singapore's Asian Aerospace '90, the RAAF's CAS (Air Marshal Ray Funnell) was actually allowed to pilot the Su-27UB. In less than two years, East-West relations had been transformed.

Le Bourget, Paris, June 1989, and the Soviet exhibits include for the first time at the Show, examples of the Soviet Air Force's latest combat aircraft. Here, the MiG-29UB *Fulcrum* sits opposite an American Gulfstream IV executive jet.
(*Tony Holmes*)

However, the airshow revelations of 1988-90 demonstrated more than the reality of Gorbachev's *glasnost*. They also brought home the fact that the traditional technology gap had disappeared, at least in airframe-engine terms.

Technology Gap

In attempting to trace how this gap has varied during the postwar years, it is tempting to concentrate on those Soviet projects that have had direct equivalents in the West, but there are dangers in such an approach.

For instance, it may appear that the gap was initially small, since the I-310 prototype for the MiG-15 flew only three months after the XP-86 Sabre, and since the transonic MiG-19 *Farmer* entered service only one year after the F-100 Super Sabre. However, the MiG-15 was nowhere

Parachute braking is used on the MiG-29, the
cruciform chute streaming from a housing between the
jetpipes. This *Fulcrum A* was one of six that visited
Finland in July 1986.

near the Sabre in terms of engine development,
equipment, and aircraft systems. Likewise, the
MiG-19 was merely a lightweight air combat
fighter (admittedly a good one for its day),
whereas the F-100 was a heavier escort fighter
that became a very useful fighter-bomber. The
fact that both had a limited supersonic capability
over a small altitude band made the two designs
directly comparable only in afterburner and
wing development. In other respects they were
very different products.

As technological progress brought longer development periods, the East–West timescale gap
at the first flight and operational deployment
stages tended to widen. The Mach 2 Ye-4 prototype for the MiG-21 *Fishbed* flew almost two
years after the XF-104 Starfighter. Likewise, the
Mach 2.8 MiG-25 *Foxbat*, that was originally
developed to counter the Rockwell XB-70, appeared about two years after the equally fast
Lockheed YF-12A. The variable-sweep Su-17
was similarly delayed relative to the F-111, but
the Sukhoi aircraft was only a swing-wing
derivative of the Su-7 (also known as *Fitter*). The
real equivalent of the F-111 is the Su-24 *Fencer*,
which flew six or seven years later than the GD
aircraft, but is more of a true fighter-bomber.

In the 1970s the MiG-29 flew three years after
the Northrop YF-17, the Su-27 five years after the
F-15, and the Su-25 five years after the A-10.
These figures suggest that a substantial gap
persisted throughout that decade. On the other
hand, the MiG-29 probably has a better wing
planform than the YF-17, the Su-27 has an FBW
control system that the F-15 lacks, and the Su-25
has a much thinner wing and higher
thrust/weight ratio (and hence a higher speed
capability) than the A-10.

A bald comparison of first flight dates for corresponding types may thus be misleading, as the aircraft cited (though basically similar) are seldom identical in terms of operational effectiveness. There is another hazard in this method, since such comparisons emphasise the significance of Soviet projects that were developed in response to (ie, either to counter or to emulate) Western aircraft. These 'reaction-type' aircraft inevitably lag behind those they respond (or correspond) to, hence such comparisons tend to overstate the Western technology lead. They also ignore areas in which the Soviets lead, such as attack helicopters (compared to West European services) and the use of CTOL aircraft from skijump-equipped carriers.

On the whole, and bearing in mind the 10 years or so now taken from go-ahead to IOC, there currently does not appear to be a significant lag in the general area of combat aircraft developments, though the relationship in avionics and armament is difficult to assess.

In the past, Soviet designers have often been portrayed in the West as mere plagiarists, whose success relied initially on German wartime developments and subsequently on copying US technology. The Soviets have unquestionably benefited in several major respects from Western work, such as early German wind tunnel research on swept wings, and the sample batch of Rolls-Royce jet engines supplied by a naive Labour government in 1947. More recently, information on the Hughes APG-65 radar of the F/A-18 is believed to have been obtained illegally by the Soviets to assist in the development of the NO-193 radar for the MiG-29.

Despite this willingness to profit from Western ideas and products, Soviet designers have also pursued some quite independent lines of development. Only they have persisted with jet-powered flying boats and amphibians, and developed really heavy long-range interceptors. Only they have put into service a Mach 2.8 interceptor. Although the upper surface blowing STOL concept was a Western idea (pioneered in the Boeing YC-14), only the Russians have developed it to production status. In the rotary-wing field, they have led in the development of a 'flying armoured personnel carrier' (ie, the Mi-24) and

perhaps in the context of air-to-air combat capability. They have certainly led in terms of both fixed- and rotary-wing aircraft that can live with front-line forces, if necessary using fuel from armoured ground vehicles. As mentioned earlier, the Soviets are far in advance of the West in using relatively conventional fighters from aircraft carriers without catapult gear.

It is arguable that we in the West should have taken more note of what was happening on the other side of the Iron Curtain, rather than arrogantly assuming that the Communists were following in our footsteps, and that Western companies need compete only with each other.

Looking at Soviet aircraft in more general terms, for at least the first two generations of jet combat aircraft their designers were significantly ahead of us in producing simple, reliable aircraft systems. Unlike ours, their fighters have to survive the harshest possible climatic conditions. They must also be able to operate from badly-surfaced runways, and continue to fly despite the ministrations of comparatively unskilled servicing and maintenance personnel.

It is noteworthy that in the case of their latest fighter, the Su-27, emphasis was placed on servicing in bad weather. Black boxes are removed downwards via the nosewheel bay, to protect both the equipment and groundcrew.

Although the ability to operate from grass has been planned for several Western combat aircraft types, only the Soviets have taken this possibility seriously. Their fighters have generally had intakes and undercarriages designed for operation not only from grass, but also from runways covered in gravel, mud or slush. Soviet basic jet trainers (notably the Czech-built L-39, developed to meet Soviet requirements) routinely operate from grass runways. For decades Soviet fighters overcame the threat of runway bombing by their ability to take off and land on specially-drained grass strips on either side of the paving.

The robustness of Soviet undercarriages is exploited by the Chinese in the use of deep gravel overruns, which (in the case of brake failure or an excessively fast landing) can bring the aircraft to rest without the need for an arrester hook, and without the airframe damage often associated with conventional barriers. If the landing was

The LIM-6 was a Polish development of the MiG-17, aimed at attaining the ability to operate from grass strips on a year-round basis. The twin mainwheels retracted into a deepened inner wing section, which had its chord extended to reduce the effect on critical Mach No.

simply misjudged, a quick visual inspection of the undercarriage is normally all that is required before the aircraft is ready to fly again.

Because of the need to be able to operate from grass, Soviet combat aircraft have generally used lower tyre pressures than their Western equivalents. This approach was taken to extreme in the case of the LIM-6 Polish variant of the MiG-17 *Fresco C*, in which the inboard wing carried a deep 'glove' on its surface to allow the use of a second wheel on either main leg. Contrary to some Western reports, several hundred LIM-6s were built, in addition to the main production run of LIM-5s (standard MiG-17s).

The likelihood of debris, mud and slush being thrown up by the wheels and into the intakes has led Soviet Bloc designers to pay special attention to protecting their engines from foreign object damage (FOD). One manifestation of this is the unique overwing intake location used for the L-39, probably the only jet trainer suited to operations from unpaved runways.

The concern with FOD probably encouraged the Soviets to retain for many years their use of nose intakes (as instanced by the MiG-15, -17, -19 and -21), despite the problems such intakes caused in regard to equipment access, radar antenna size, and accomodating a multi-camera package.

More recent Soviet combat aircraft employ lateral intakes, primarily to allow a large nose radome. One disadvantage of such inlets is that they may ingest debris, water, slush, etc, that is thrown up by the nosewheels, even if they are fitted with mudguards. In two recent cases Soviet designers have gone to quite extraordinary lengths to protect their engines during ground operations, accepting significant weight penalties and a drop in take-off performance. In the case of the MiG-29, the main intakes are closed by means of doors during take-off and landing, and the engines are supplied with air from auxiliary inlets in the upper wing surface.

As the result of the growing number of Western pilots who have been allowed to fly in the MiG-29U (with some operational equipment switched off), a certain amount has been learned about the use of these inlet guards, although the Soviets are still not completely open on this subject. Probably the most informative such demonstration was that given by Mikoyan chief test pilot Valery Menitsky to John Farley, formerly chief test pilot for British Aerospace at Dunsfold, and the man largely responsible for the flight test development of the V/STOL Sea Harrier.

One of the more bizarre of early Soviet jet fighter projects was the Lavochkin La-200 series, powered by two centrifugal-flow engines in tandem in the fuselage. Both engines received air from the nose intake, but the forward unit exhausted under the centre fuselage, while the rear unit exhausted under the tail. The La-200B (above) used three separate intakes, with the lowest feeding the front engine. First flight took place in 1952. The concept lost out to the more conventional Yak-25, with wing-mounted engines.

By Farley's account (much of which was published in *Flight International*) the position of the two intake doors is displayed in the cockpit in the form of vertical strip indicators relatively low down on the right side of the main instrument panel, with the scales reading 0 to 100 per cent. Farley had been briefed that the doors would be fully open by the time that an airspeed of 108 knots (200 km/hr) had been achieved. However, it was subsequently established that the restrictions allow the MiG-29 to be flown as fast as 430 knots (800 km/hr) with the main doors fully closed, provided that AOA is then limited to 22 degrees (presumably because intake drag significantly reduces directional stability).

When Farley asked what were the factors that signalled the doors to open or close, he was told 'engine pressures, temperatures and outside conditions'. It was clear that the decision process is far more complicated than airspeed and weight on the oleos, and that it had been arrived at as the

result of a great deal of testing. Two points worth emphasising are that Farley praised the smooth thrust growth from idle to maximum reheat, and noted that the pilot could override the automatic control system and select the intake doors closed in high-speed low level flight, if he saw that he was approaching a flock of birds.

To digress briefly (before leaving the subject of the MiG-29), it is also noteworthy that Farley felt that the aircraft has had so much effort poured into refining its low speed handling characteristics that it is actually easier to fly (slow) than a Jet Provost. Although there are rigid G-limits (9.5G, reducing to 7G above Mach 0.85, though individual display pilots may be cleared to 10.5G), there is no such restriction on AOA at speeds below Mach 0.85 (above which it is 15°). There is a control column restriction introduced at an AOA of 30°, reduced by 0.3 times the rate of increase of AOA, but this can be overriden. The key to good handling at high AOA appears to be the precise control of vortex flows (eg, by adding small strakes at the base of the nose-probe) and the gradual blending of lateral control contributions. Below 8.7° AOA, lateral control is provided by a combination of ailerons and differential tailplane. Between 8.7° and 20.5°, down-going aileron inputs are gradually reduced, and rudder movement is phased in. Beyond 8.7°, the leading edge flaps are automatically extended, and there is no differential tailplane movement.

The MiG-9 *Fargo* was the production version of the I-300, which was the first turbojet-powered fighter of Soviet design to fly. Its maiden flight took place on 24 April 1946, only shortly before that of the Yak-15, the right to fly first having been won by the toss of a coin.

The measures taken to protect the engines of the Su-27 are less radical, but nonetheless unique. In this case the main intakes remain in use while on the ground, but stones and birds (though not water) are excluded by titanium grills that are retracted out of the way during flight. There is also a reference in Su-27 literature to a 'blowaway jet system' to protect the intakes, presumably by destroying the foot of any vortex rising from the ground to the inlet.

Soviet operational requirements appear to place emphasis on aircraft simplicity and reliability, due to the comparatively low educational standard of groundcrew conscripts. For the same reason, automatic checkout equipment is employed very extensively, even for simple basic jet trainers such as the L-39. For deployment to forward operating sites, the Su-25 *Frogfoot* can take four pylon-mounted pods to make it self-sufficient (aside from fuel supplies), and one of these contains automatic test equipment (ATE).

Soviet day fighters of the 1950s and '60s were very reliable aircraft, with reportedly smaller needs for servicing and maintenance than their Western equivalents. One innovation in this area was the development of modification kits with 'one-shot' special tools that were simply thrown away after use. However, the Soviet approach to maintenance does not appear to have changed much over the past 40 years. In the West such work has been rationalized to avoid wherever

A foreshortened view of the two Su-27 *Flankers* that appeared in public for the first time at Paris 1989. Below the red star national marking is the Sukhoi Design Bureau insignia.
(*Tony Holmes*)

possible such pointless exercises as stripping down perfectly serviceable components on a rigid schedule, and creating defects in the process. It may be recalled that in the 1970s British Aerospace and Rolls-Royce were contracted by the Egyptian Air Force to establish completely new maintenance programmes for the MiG-21 and its engine.

It is also doubtful whether the Soviets have equalled the West in the dramatic improvements in avionics reliability achieved during the 1970s and '80s. A simply-equipped aircraft such as the Su-25 *Frogfoot* may thus have a better MTBF (mean time between failures) than the A-10, but

the reliability of a sophisticated dual-role aircraft such as the MiG-29 is probably not as good as that for the F/A-18. It may be noted that in April 1990 the West German Air Force ruled out the idea of using MiG-29s as a substitute for the Eurofighter EFA in a unified *Luftwaffe*, partly because of the suspect reliability of the MiG.

Soviet combat aircraft have tended to differ from ours partly because of their different war-time experience of air operations. One major difference was that the Soviets emerged from WW2 with little experience of strategic bombing. On the other hand they were probably second to none in terms of close support and ground attack, having led in the use of heavily-armoured rocket-firing aircraft. The use of the Ilyushin Il-2 *Bark* and the subsequent Il-10 *Beast* as airborne tank-destroyers ('as essential to the Red Army as air and bread') encouraged an emphasis on numerical strength and compatibility with front-line operations. This background led to persistent postwar demands for aircraft of comparative simplicity and low cost, features that could be attained only at some sacrifice in overall effectiveness.

The ability to live with forward army units is well illustrated by the cases of the Su-25 and Mi-28. In emergency the engines of the Su-25 can be operated for 24 hours on army diesel fuel, and this may also be true for the Mi-28. The latter is also noteworthy for its extremely low tyre pressures, and its use of a standard Red Army 30 mm cannon from the BMP-2 armoured personnel carrier. In such respects these are far more down-to-earth products than America's A-10 and AH-64.

It is also noteworthy that experience in Afghanistan during the 1980s has encouraged a very serious approach to vulnerability-reduction through foam-filled tanks, armour plate, and the installation of very large numbers of chaff/flare dispensers. The Su-25 is a far more survivable aircraft than (say) a Harrier, though the latter is admittedly far less likely to be hit, due to its small size and high speed.

The influence of WW 2 in encouraging the development of lightweight, low-cost aircraft that could be afforded in large numbers was

There are few radars in service that can match the performance of the Hughes APG-70 pulse-Doppler set carried by the McDonnell Douglas F-15 Eagle and it is certainly some years ahead of the system currently in the Su-27. (*Dennis Baldry*)

probably a good thing for the first fighter generation, aimed at the daylight clear weather point defence and short-range air superiority roles. However, as demands grew for more capable fighters, with supersonic performance, day/night all-weather capability, and the flexibility to switch to the ground attack role, this tradition of lightweight combat aircraft arguably held the Soviets back. The MiG-21, though featuring some bold innovations, thus acquired a reputation as a 'goes nowhere, does nothing aeroplane'. Such criticisms brought a watershed in Soviet fighter development, and the MiG-21 was superseded by the much heavier and more capable MiG-23/27 *Flogger*. Continuing this theme, it is noteworthy that the Soviet equivalent of the F-16 is the much larger, twin-engined MiG-29. The time when capability could be restricted in the pursuit of vast numbers is long past.

After quite severe performance deficiencies with the prototype Su-27 (designated T-10 by Sukhoi), a major redesign was put in hand and the resulting aircraft is now a formidable air defence fighter.
(*Tony Holmes*)

The early Soviet obsession with low unit costs, coupled with the belief (not entirely shared in the West) that warplanes should be designed for war rather than peace, was probably responsible for the relatively short lives of their combat aircraft and engines. Figures for the operating lives of current Soviet types have not yet been published, but some indication of those for earlier generations may be provided by Chinese-built aircraft of Soviet design.

For example, the Guizhou FT-7 supersonic fighter-trainer, based on the MiG-21U *Mongol A*, has a total service life (with overhauls at 600 hr intervals) of 1800 hr. Its WP-7MB engine has a life of 600 hr, probably implying a TBO of 200 hr. For comparison, Western combat aircraft have service lives of 3000–6000 hr, and most Western military engines now have module inspection periods of 500 hr upwards.

To offset the short lives of Soviet combat aircraft, they are operated far less intensively than those in the West. According to the Pentagon document *Soviet Military Power 1985* (SMP-85), a Soviet pilot is supposed to make 180 sorties each year to maintain proficiency. However, due to the relatively short endurance of most Soviet tactical aircraft to date (which may be regarded as another result of designing for low

cost), 180 sorties correspond to an annual total of only 80–120 flying hours. For comparison, the NATO target is 240 hr, a figure that is attained by the average USAF combat pilot. His opposite number in the USN/USMC reportedly flies 300 hr, a figure that reflects the long endurance of carrier-based aircraft.

To compensate for what can only be regarded as a very limited amount of flying by each pilot, Soviet training (again quoting from SMP-85) 'emphasises extensive pre-flight preparation and post-flight evaluation of mission sorties'. In addition, whereas NATO pilots generally have new postings at two or three year intervals, including desk jobs that prepare them for staff duties, the Soviet philosophy is to concentrate on 'continuity in flying assignments and flying the same aircraft for a long time'. The fact that Soviet aircrew have to sign on for 25 years clearly helps to establish a core of well-experienced pilots.

Like the F-15 Eagle, the Su-27 has a large hydraulically-operated dorsal airbrake for use in flight or, as shown here by the two-seat version, for shortening the landing run.
(*Tony Holmes*)

Design Characteristics

In some respects Soviet combat aircraft developments appear to have mirrored those in the UK, though perhaps with fewer major programme cancellations. One fundamental reason for this similarity has been the geographic proximity of enemy nuclear bomber bases. The Soviet Union and Britain both lacked the long warning times that were provided for North America by the NORAD system, which allowed the US to concentrate on slow-climbing long-range escort fighters such as the F-86 and F-100. In consequence the RAF and SAF (strictly speaking, the PVO or Air Defence Force, which was traditionally a separate service) have needed defending aircraft that can climb quickly to the bomber's altitude and then accelerate to provide the most distant possible intercept.

The result has been a series of fighters in which thrust/weight ratio was emphasized at the expense of fuel fraction, ie, they had a lot of engine and consequently little fuel. This description applied to British aircraft such as the Hunter and Lightning, and to Soviet aircraft such as the MiG-21 and Su-7.

Another similarity was that only Britain and the Soviet Union developed fighters with highly

The *Fishpot* designation was applied initially to the Su-9 series, but from 1966 this was replaced on the production line by the Su-11, which was basically similar but introduced a more powerful engine, an enlarged intake, a later radar, and a missile armament of two AA-3 *Anabs* in place of four AA-1 *Alkalis*.

swept wings (using this description in a delta-excluding sense), namely the Lightning, Su-7 and Ye-2A *Faceplate*. It is possible that both nations adopted this dead-end in wing planform development simply because they lagged in the manufacturing techniques required by lighter (though thinner) wings of moderate sweep.

The Su-7 and the Mikoyan bureau's Ye-2A were very similar configurations, as was the case with the Su-9/11 *Fishpot* and MiG-21. The advent of near-identical designs from different bureaus (right up to the current similarity of MiG-29 and Su-27) has been a uniquely Soviet characteristic, indicating the crucial role of Moscow's Central Fluid Dynamics Institute (TsAGI), which is now headed by Guerman I Zagainov.

This organization is broadly comparable to America's NASA and Britain's RAE, but it appears to have been far more influential in practical terms, perhaps simply because Soviet industry lacks its own major wind tunnels. According to their historians, a group was formed at TsAGI in 1942 under Sedov to investigate supersonic aerodynamics, and four years later a group was established under Struminsky to research the near-term demands of transonic flow. It is also claimed that TsAGI researchers formulated Area Rule as early as 1945–46, more than 10 years before Dick Whitcomb of NASA. Whether or not this is true, it was certainly clear

Soviet air shows have never been plentiful, so when they have been held interest from the West is guaranteed. This one was at Domodedovo in 1967. The line-up shows (from the bottom) a Mil Mi-1 *Hare*, Myasishchev M-4 *Bison C*, Tu-16 *Badger*, Yak-28P *Firebar*, Su-7 *Fitter A*, Mikoyan Ye-166, MiG-21 *Fishbed* and An-14 *Clod*. On the far left are some preserved Second World War types.

from this writer's conversation with Professor Pavlenko of TsAGI in 1968 that the organization is tasked with developing configurational options for future combat aircraft. It is, however, noteworthy that the Sukhoi bureau claims responsibility for the Su-27 configuration, which is said to have been leaked to the Mikoyan bureau via TsAGI.

One of the better features of the Soviet system has been the willingness to fund research aircraft and technology demonstrators, and (more recently) to carry out extended service trials with radically new aircraft types. Examples of their research aircraft include the Mikoyan bureau's Ye-166 and the Su-100 Mach 3 aircraft that flew in 1972. In the early 1960s, the Ye-166 established several world records, including a 15/25 km closed circuit speed of 2681 km/hr (approx 1675 mph) and a sustained altitude of 22,670 m (approx 74,350 ft).

In the mid-1950s the Mikoyan and Sukhoi bureaus constructed a number of technology demonstrators to make direct comparisons of highly swept wings and tailed-delta configurations. The latter concept was virtually a Soviet

invention, though it was also used for the Messerschmitt/Hispano HA-300 and BAC's TSR.2 strike aircraft. The Soviets evidently concluded from their trials that the two configurations were fairly evenly matched, since the highly swept wing went into service on the Su-7, while the tailed-delta was used for the MiG-21 and Su-9/11.

An even more significant use of technology demonstrators occurred in the mid/late 1960s, when the Soviets were making efforts to reduce airfield requirements. The V/STOL Harrier had completed transitions between jet-borne and wing-borne flight in 1961, and the Soviets were evidently not keen to develop a dedicated vectored-thrust engine such as the Pegasus to achieve a reduction in field lengths. For the STOL performance that interested them, less revolutionary concepts would suffice. On the one hand, they could use variable-sweep wings, providing much more aerodynamic lift than had been possible with highly swept or small delta wings. Alternatively, they could use special lift engines (similar to those successfully developed by Rolls-Royce) to support about half the aircraft weight at take-off and landing.

At the Domodedovo airshow of July 1967, a whole range of swing-wing and lift engine technology demonstrators were flown. One important newcomer was the Ye-231, the prototype for the MiG-23, using a variable-sweep wing to provide direct comparison with the same

---

Sukhoi's attempt at designing a supersonic, long-range jet bomber was the Su-100. The nose drooped and so did the programme; it now resides at the Soviet Air Force museum at Monino.

bureau's Ye-230 *Faithless* which had two lift engines in the centre fuselage. These two aircraft had virtually identical fuselages and tails, but the Ye-230 had a delta wing and semi-conical intakes, whereas the swing-wing Ye-231 had two-dimensional inlets, Phantom-style.

A less direct comparison was provided by a MiG-21 *Fishbed G* equipped with two lift engines, and the variable-sweep S-221 prototype for the Su-17 *Fitter C*. The largest of the STOL aircraft on show was the Su-15VD *Flagon B*, which had three of these lift engines developed by Koliesov.

At the lower end of the weight range, two examples of the V-STOL Yak-36 *Freehand* were shown, each with two lift engines installed horizontally in the lower front fuselage, exhausting through rotatable nozzles under the CG. The concept derived from the Bell X-14, which was the world's first practical vectored-thrust aircraft. The nature of these various lift engine installations suggested that the Koliesov design produced about 50 per cent more thrust than the RB.162, and roughly the same as the R-R/Allison XJ99, the first example of which ran in 1968. With hindsight, this prediction was somewhat on the high side, since the XJ99 was in the 9000 lb (4080 kg) class, while the Soviet lift engine is reportedly rated at 7875 lb (3570 kg), ie 12.5 per cent less.

In principle, the Yak-36 could have been used as the basis for a V/STOL close support and tactical reconnaissance aircraft. However, from this writer's subsequent conversation with Soviet designers working in the V/STOL field, it was clear that they had been presented with a draft OR following helicopter practice, with a hot, high VTO, and demanding the ability to operate from grass without surface preparation. This latter aspect of the requirement was virtually impossible to satisfy, and it was evidently concluded that a fixed-wing V/STOL aircraft was not the way to go, at least as far as ground-based operations were concerned. The first Mi-24 attack helicopter flew about four years after that conversation.

For their STOL programmes, they meanwhile concluded that the swing-wing was the best solution. The decisive factors were probably simplicity (compared to the use of lift engines), reliability, a lower weight penalty, low drag, and high penetration speed. This decision led to the production of the Su-17 and MiG-23/27, and later to the progressively larger Su-24 *Fencer*, Tu-22M *Backfire* and Tu-160 *Blackjack*. The introduction of the Su-17 and MiG-27 also signalled a move to genuine fighter-bombers with worthwhile warload-radius performance. Prior to this generation, ground attack had generally been left to aircraft that had been designed as short-range interceptors, but with time had fallen behind current standards in climb performance and maximum speed.

Service Trials

The Soviet willingness to undertake extensive service trials was illustrated by the appearance of the Yak-38 *Forger* VTOL aircraft on the *Kiev* anti-submarine aircraft carrier in 1976. This aircraft was later based on three subsequent ships of this class (the *Minsk*, *Novorossiysk*, and *Baku*), and it is believed that around 75 have been built. The Yak-38 clearly has only a very limited capability for daylight air defence, close support and reconnaissance, in addition to which it might provide mid-course guidance for ship-to-ship missiles. However, the absence of any external evidence of significant operational equipment indicates that these aircraft have merely been used to accumulate experience of operating VTOL aircraft at sea. The benefit of this will presumably be seen in the Yak-41, which is expected to become the world's first production supersonic V/STOL aircraft.

Large-scale operational trials of new concepts were later to be illustrated by the use of the Su-25 *Frogfoot* in Afghanistan, where two squadrons of these relatively low speed but highly manoeuvrable aircraft were tested over a period of several years. The survivability of this aircraft was undoubtedly improved by a large factor as a result of the modifications introduced during that conflict (mainly to reduce losses due to the Blowpipe, Redeye and Stinger man-portable SAMs), but whether the Soviets would now commit such aircraft in Central Europe is still not clear. It should also be mentioned at this point that several other types of Soviet aircraft benefited from the Afghanistan experience, including helicopters and transports. Aside from the lavish use of cartridge-type dispensers, infrared jammers have also been introduced on most support and attack helicopters.

Four Generations

One point that emerges quite clearly from a study of Soviet developments since WW2 is that important new fighters have appeared in a series of distinct waves, separated by intervals of approximately 10 years. The first postwar generation of note introduced swept wings, and was exemplified by the MiG-15 *Fagot* and the technically interesting (though far less important) Lavochkin La-15 *Fantail*, which appeared in 1947–48. The theme was taken further by the aerodynamically improved MiG-17 *Fresco*, which introduced the use of an afterburner, and the marginally transonic twin-engined MiG-19 *Farmer*.

The first 10 postwar years also saw the advent of the twin-engined, radar-equipped two-seat Yak-25 *Flashlight* night fighter. In the bomber field, this initial period witnessed the arrival of

the straight-wing Il-28 *Beagle* light bomber, the swept-wing Tu-16 *Badger* and M-4 *Bison* medium bombers, and that remarkable swept-wing turboprop, the Tu-95 *Bear*. This last aircraft was still in production in the late 1980s as a platform for long-range cruise missiles.

The second generation of Soviet jet fighters appeared in 1956 in the form of their first Mach 2 aircraft: the prototypes for the MiG-21, Su-7 and Su-9. By the early 1960s the Yak-25 was being replaced by the supersonic Yak-28 *Firebar* and the Tu-28 *Fiddler*, the heaviest fighter ever

Soviet experiments with VTOL resulted in production of the Yak-38 *Forger* which, although limited in capability, has given the Soviet Navy experience in operating this type of fixed-wing aircraft. These three examples have the doors of their lift engines open and the nearest machine carries a 23 mm gun pod.

produced. Around 1964 the highly capable Su-15 *Flagon* and the Mach 2.8 MiG-25 made their first flights. Meanwhile the bomber version of the Yak-28 (*Brewer*) and the much heavier Tu-22 *Blinder* had entered service.

In the third generation, Soviet fighters combined high supersonic speeds with STOL capability, though their ground runs might more accurately be described as reduced, rather than short. The MiG-23 and Su-17 were ready in prototype form for the great Domodedovo airshow of 1967, and by 1970 the Su-24 *Fencer* and Tu-22M *Backfire* had flown, all with variable sweep-wings. In 1973-74 the VTOL Yak-38 *Forger* made its first flight. At that stage attempts to develop a VTOL close support aircraft for the land battle had been abandoned, but that role was taken on by the combination of the Mi-24 *Hind* helicopter and the fixed-wing Su-25 *Frogfoot*, which provided a reasonable STOL performance.

For their fourth generation, the Soviets followed the US in aiming for far higher manoeuvrability in air combat, coupled with a look-down, shoot down capability. These aircraft are indirect results of the Vietnam War, in which the kill-ratio had at times been only marginally in favour of the US. America therefore needed a quantum leap in specific excess power and turning performance to ensure air supremacy in future conflicts, and the Soviets felt obliged to respond. The resulting Su-27 *Flanker* and MiG-29 *Fulcrum* both left the ground in 1977. In the strategic bomber category, the Tu-160 *Blackjack* had its maiden flight in 1980/81. The Mi-28 *Havoc* attack helicopter flew in 1982, just over 10 years after the pioneering Mi-24.

The remarkable regularity of the appearance of new Soviet fighter generations (the swept-wing MiG-15 in 1947, the Mach 2 MiG-21 in 1956/57, the variable-geometry MiG-23 in 1966/67, and the highly manoeuvrable MiG-29 in 1977) suggests that prototypes for a fifth generation might have been anticipated in 1986/87. However, with the sole exception of the Yak-41 supersonic V/STOL aircraft that is believed to be under development for the *Tbilisi*-class carriers, there appears to be no photographic evidence that Soviet fifth-generation fighters really exist.

Summary

Reviewing four generations of postwar Soviet combat aircraft, they got off to a good start by maintaining a wartime development momentum, and by exploiting German aerodynamics and British turbojet technology. Nonetheless, throughout most of this period Soviet fighters have lagged behind the best of Western products by an average approaching five years. Recently, during the 1980s, the chronological airframe gap (which is the most visible measure of performance) appears to have been reduced to a size that is no longer significant, bearing in mind that aircraft may remain in service for 20–30 years.

Ironically, although we have tended to take it for granted that the Soviets lag behind in avionics and missiles, it was they who pioneered the use of EO sensors and laser ranging in air combat, producing a much stealthier search-and-track device than radar, and a major improvement in the accuracy of air-to-air gunnery. Whether such devices are also intended to blind opposing pilots has yet to be established, but the potential is there.

It is arguable that most Soviet aviation innovations (eg Mach 2.8 interceptors, long-range swept-wing turboprops, jet-powered flying boats, and large ram-wings and other surface-cushion vehicles) are merely exploiting areas of technology that the US has deliberately chosen to ignore. It might also be argued that Soviet combat aircraft will tend to be inferior to their American equivalents, simply because Communism emphasizes conformity, whereas the entire history of US technology is based on a national ability to innovate (and the reward of innovators).

There may be some truth in both of these contentions, but it would be foolhardy in the extreme to write off the new generation of Soviet designers (such as Mikhail Petrovitch Simonov of the Sukhoi bureau) as simple-minded plagiarists, who are condemned by their education and upbringing to spend their lives trailing along behind their Western equivalents. Looking at the Su-27, this writer would hope that when the fifth generation of Soviet combat aircraft eventuates, men such as Simonov are working with us, rather than against us.

2 The Subsonic/Transonic Generation

In spite of the decades that have passed since the earliest Soviet jet combat aircraft flew, this first generation retains considerable significance, since it provided the springboard for the later generations, and since some of these old aircraft are still in widespread use.

Substantial numbers of the MiG-15UTI, MiG-17, MiG-19, Il-28 and Tu-16 remain in operation around the world. The Chinese F-4, F-6 and A-5 are all based on first-generation Soviet designs. The *Bear H* cruise missile-carrying version of the Tu-95 remained in production until the late 1980s, and other variants remain in use for maritime patrol, ASW, and ELINT duties. Beginning in 1986, small numbers of flyable MiG-15s, MiG-15UTI's and MiG-17s have been imported from China and Poland to the US, UK and Australia. (Some MiG-21s and F-7s have also recently become available from various countries, but these aircraft belong to the second generation).

Jet Propulsion

The Soviet Union (like the US) lagged behind Britain and Germany in the early development of gas turbines for aircraft propulsion. However, it was widely recognized in the late 1930s that the combination of piston engine and unducted propeller would have an eventual speed restriction of about 500 mph (800 km/hr). What was needed was a new form of propulsion, with a power output that increased with speed, and that avoided the normal drop in efficiency associated with the propeller blade tips approaching Mach 1.

Gas turbines had already been developed for ground-based electrical power applications, but the concept was felt to offer little short-term potential for aircraft propulsion. The main problems were low compressor and turbine efficiencies, and the lack of turbine materials suited to the high temperatures needed for good thermodynamic efficiency.

The obvious conclusion (unless you were Whittle or von Ohain) was that the long-term future rested with jet propulsion in some form that avoided the problems of the gas turbine. The possibilities included the piston-driven ducted-fan (as in the Caproni-Campini research aircraft), the ramjet (patented by Lorin in France) and the liquid-fuel rocket (developed by Walter in Germany).

The first Soviet aircraft application of jet thrust was probably represented by trials in 1934–35, in which up to six solid fuel rockets were used to improve the take-off performance of a Tupolev I-4 (ANT-5) sesquiplane. However, Soviet historians state that design work on the Lyukla VRD-1 axial-flow turbojet began in 1938. It continued until the German invasion of 1941, when development efforts were switched to programmes promising quick results.

In the meanwhile, various trials had begun in which small ramjets were employed as boost motors. The programme included a 1940 test using a Polikarpov I-153DM biplane, which experienced a speed increase of 26 mph (42 km/hr). Experiments later took place with a modified La-7, and the La-9RD. The 1946 Tushino flypast included a formation of La-9RDs, each with two underwing ramjets.

The first Soviet aircraft to be powered solely

Two MiG-15 *Fagots*, one Czech and the other Polish, operating in an early Warsaw Pact exercise. In Korea, the performance of this clear-weather interceptor came as a surprise to the Allies.

by a jet engine was the Bereznyak-Isayev BI-1, which was also the world's first rocket-powered fighter. Dushkin had successfully demonstrated a liquid-fuel rocket motor in 1939. Some of these tests were witnessed by an aircraft design engineer named Bereznyak, who subsequently collaborated (within the Bolkhovinitov OKB) with Isayev from the Dushkin team on the design of the BI-1. It had its first powered flight on 15 May 1942, some 15 months ahead of Germany's Me 163.

The BI-1 had a gross weight of 3710 lb (1683 kg) and was powered by a D-1A motor, burning kerosene with nitric acid as oxidant. The D-1A gave a maximum thrust of 2424 lb (1100 kg) for 80 seconds, taking the BI-1 to 32,800 ft (10,000 m) in a remarkable 59 seconds. The BI-1 was armed with two 20 mm ShVAK cannon. Plans for an initial production batch of 50 aircraft

were, however, abandoned after the BI-1 disintegrated on its seventh flight, following a sudden nose-down pitch, probably caused by shock-induced flow separations.

The same type of rocket had also been used in two unsuccessful competitors: the Tikhonravov I-302 and the Polikarpov *Malyutka* (Little One) The I-302 had a mixed powerplant, combining the D-1A rocket with two underwing ramjets for cruise.

The smaller Glushko RD-1 rocket was tested as a boost motor on the Yak-3, Petlyakov Pe-2RD, Su-6 and La-7. With an uprated piston engine the La-7R was redesignated La-120R, and this aircraft was presented at Tushino in 1946.

Acquisition by the Soviets of the Me 263/Ju 248 at the end of the war sparked off a brief revival of interest in pure rocket fighters, their high climb rates being particularly attractive in the new vital task of intercepting nuclear bombers. The MiG bureau produced the I-270(ZhRD), which was rather like a plump Bell X-1, though with a T-tail. It first flew in late 1946, but was written off in the course of flight tests.

The Russian abbreviation ZhRD indicated a liquid-fuel rocket motor, the other common abbreviations being PD for piston engine, TRD for turbojet, TVD for turboprop, and PVRD for ramjet.

As a stepping-stone to the turbojet, while avoiding the high temperature problems of the turbine, TsIAM (the Central Institute for Aero-Engines) developed the 'Accelerator'. This used a forward-mounted 1700 hp VK-107 piston engine to turn both a propeller and a compressor that supplied air to a combustion chamber and nozzle in the rear fuselage. The jet thrust was approximately 660 lb (300 kg).

In the spring of 1944 the Sukhoi and MiG bureaus were ordered to design single-seat fighters around this powerplant. The resulting Su-5

reached 503 mph (810 km/hr) at 32,800 ft (10,000 m), but was not produced in series. The MiG bureau's I-250(N) flew on 2 March 1945 and reached 513 mph (825 km/hr) at 25,600 ft (7800 m). A small batch served with Naval Aviation as the MiG-13.

The Real Thing

Arkhip Lyulka, 'the father of gas turbines in the Soviet Union', followed his VRD-1 study with bench-testing of the 1543 lb (700 kg) VRD-2, and with full-scale development of the 2865 lb (1300 kg) VRD-3, which received the service designation TR-1. This was the first air-breathing Soviet jet engine to be used as the sole means of propulsion for an aircraft.

The TR-1 is claimed to have completed testbed running by the end of 1944, though it first appeared three years later in the four-engined

America's answer to the MiG-15 was the North American F-86 Sabre. These are F-86F versions pictured just prior to the Armistice in 1953.

Il-22 bomber, which flew in July 1947 and was shown at Tushino in the following month. The TR-1 was also employed in the twin-engined Su-11 fighter, which was exhibited at Tushino in 1948.

Despite the claimed availability of the Lyulka TR-1, all early production Soviet jet aircraft relied on the RD-10 (Junkers Jumo 004 copy) or the RD-20 (BMW 003 copy). The situation changed from 1947 with the advent of the RD-500 (Rolls-Royce Derwent copy) and the RD-45 (R-R Nene copy). The first Soviet-designed engine of operational significance was the VK-1, a R-R Nene derivative, roughly equivalent to the British company's Tay. It was these German and British engines that kept Soviet jet fighters flying until 1952–53, when the first fully indigenous and worthwhile Soviet turbojets appeared on the scene.

The purpose of the first Soviet jet fighters was to replace Lavochkin's radial-engined La-9 and -11, and Yakovlev's liquid-cooled Yak-9 and -3. By the middle of the war, British and American designers had progressed to relatively heavy fighter-bombers with engines of 2000–2500 hp, but the Soviets still used small airframes with a 1700 hp liquid-cooled engine or an 1850 hp radial. Nonetheless, the postwar La-11 managed a commendable 459 mph (735 km/hr). Some Soviet fighter variants were fitted with heavy cannon that made them useful for strafing tanks, but close support was largely the preserve of the dedicated armoured attack aircraft, the *Shturmovik*.

For their first turbojet fighter, the SAF is believed to have considered initially the Me 262, but in early 1945 it was decided to issue requirements for two indigenous types. A single-engined fighter based on the 2000 lb (910 kg) RD-10 would thus be complemented by a twin-engined aircraft using the smaller 1760 lb (800 kg) RD-20.

By modern standards the RD-10 might produce a useful thrust for a basic trainer, but it gave less than half the thrust of the 4520 lb (2050 kg) Orpheus used in the West's lightest jet fighter, the Folland Gnat, which had a clean gross of 7800 lb (3540 kg). It was therefore natural that Yakovlev should base his single-engine sub-

mission (which became the Yak-15) on the airframe of the lightweight Yak-3. As with many other jet conversions of that period, the piston engine was simply replaced by the turbojet, which was inclined so that it exhausted below the rear fuselage, though the tailwheel undercarriage was retained.

Interestingly, the only other direct jet conversion to reach production was the Saab J21R. This was a more natural choice for conversion, since the piston original (the J21A) had a tricycle undercarriage, pod-and-booms (Vampire-type) layout, and an ejection seat.

Flight trials of the Yak-15 were delayed to allow power-on tests with the prototype in a full-scale wind tunnel, a technique used decades later with the YAV-8B Harrier II at NASA's Ames facility. The Yak-15 had its maiden flight on 24 April 1946, just after the twin-engined MiG-9, and five months ahead of the competing La-150. Both the Yak-15 and the MiG-9 flew at Tushino on 18 August 1946, when (legend has it) Stalin decreed that a dozen of each should fly past during the October parade. By an incredible effort, all 12 Yak-15s were completed by October 21st, but the flypast was cancelled due to fog.

The Yak-15 had a gross weight of 5820 lb (2640 kg), and a maximum speed of about 435 knots (805 km/hr) at sea level. Despite its limited performance and tailwheel layout, it entered service in 1947, and 300–400 were built. It was clearly only a stopgap measure, though it may have been viewed also as an insurance against failure of the MiG-9. Its practical attractions were low cost, ease of manufacture, and a cockpit very similar to that of the Yak-3. This similarity must have been an important factor for a pilot firing off a turbojet for the first time, and experiencing the strange sensations of feeble acceleration on the ground and a rapidly-unwinding fuel gauge.

The loser in the contest had been the La-150, a completely new design with all the 'jet' features the Yak-15 lacked. It had a tricycle undercarriage, and the pilot well forward, with the engine behind him. A pod-and-boom layout was used to reduce jetpipe losses, and the wing was set high, producing an excess of dihedral effect, which was later cured by turning down the tips.

A transonic replacement for the MiG-15 involved a redesign that produced the MiG-17 *Fresco*. Among the variants was the MiG-17PF *Fresco D* fitted with *Izumrud* (Emerald) AI radar for limited all-weather use, an East German-operated example seen here.

At least one of the five prototypes was flown with an afterburner at a later stage (July 1947), making this the first Soviet aircraft with reheat.

The demand for a twin-engined fighter led to a contest between the MiG-9 and Su-9. Preliminary work on the MiG-9 had assumed the use of two Lyulka VRD-3s, but in 1945 a switch was made to the far less powerful RD-20s. Whereas the single-engined fighters were to have only two 23 mm cannon, the twins were to also have one 37 mm, producing a curious mix of ballistics that reappeared in the Korean War MiG-15. The prototype of the MiG-9 was designated I-300, and first flew on 24 April 1946. The MiG-9 thus became the first Soviet jet fighter to fly, and the first production Soviet fighter with a nosewheel undercarriage.

The MiG-9 had what was to become a conventional jet layout, with a mid-set powerplant and a forward cockpit. It also had a mid-set wing, which made possible wing-mounted main undercarriage units. Strangely, these were mounted close in to the fuselage and retracted outboard, which reduced wheel track and engine access. With a clean gross weight of 11,180 lb (5070 kg), the MiG-9 was comparable to the original Gloster Meteor. It could reach 490 knots (911 km/hr) at 5000 ft (1500 m), and had a service ceiling of 42,650 ft (13,000 m). Around 1000 were built, making it the first numerically-significant Soviet jet fighter. A number of two-seat MiG-9UTIs were also produced and some were employed in early ejection seat tests.

The competing Su-9, effectively a straight-wing redesign of the Me 262, appeared slightly later. It offered more fuel volume, and thus better range and endurance, but it was heavier and slower, and (like the Meteor) posed severe engine-out handling problems. The Su-9 was not ordered into production, but it did have some interesting features, including an ejection seat, a braking parachute, and provisions for two JATO rockets. To digress, Soviet combat aircraft have retained JATO provisions to the present day, whereas the concept was abandoned many years ago in the West.

Preliminary Pointers

The period of transition from pistons to jets was technically an interesting phase of fighter development, as it required great flexibility from the

---

The British Rolls-Royce Nene centrifugal turbojet first powered Mikoyan's I-310 into the air and a Soviet development of the engine, the Klimov VK-1, became the standard powerplant for the improved MiG-15*bis*.

---

designers. The MiG bureau, which had been successful mainly in the early part of the war, experienced a strong revival, again living up to its slogan 'Speed and Altitude'. The Yakovlev team would also survive, though its jet designs were to be characterized by a certain crudity. The Lavochkin projects were visually attractive, but perhaps emphasized aerodynamics at the expense of other considerations. That team would soon disappear, as (for a time) would that of Pavel Sukhoi.

The low thrust engines of these first jet fighters encouraged a continuation of the Soviet wartime theme of lightweight fighters with little ground attack capability. The Yak-15 and MiG-9 were less flexible operationally and had less development potential than (say) the F-80 and Meteor.

The early Soviet jets also demonstrated the willingness to adopt foreign ideas and products.

In the immediate postwar period this attitude extended to recruiting German and Austrian personnel, who contributed significantly to Soviet combat aircraft design until at least the early 1950s. Some then returned home, but others, having raised families in the Soviet Union and having no aircraft industry to return to, elected to stay.

The German influence probably supported the use of simple nose intakes, whereas Western designers moved quickly to lateral inlets. Although the latter introduced boundary layer problems, they saved weight and reduced the size of the vertical tail. As noted earlier, they also made available far more equipment space in the front fuselage for radar, camera arrays, etc. Although some early Soviet jet fighters were equipped with reconnaissance cameras, there was to be no real equivalent of the Hunter FR10 or the RF-84F. Tactical reconnaissance was largely to be left to heavier twin-engined types such as the Yak-28 *Brewer*.

The early Soviet designs also generally followed German wartime practice in using fin-mounted tailplanes, although these aggravated compressibility problems and (later) the pitch-up tendency of swept-back wings. However, the Soviets were initially cautious in following the Germans in the adoption of swept wings, a point underlined by the straight-wing Su-9 following the swept-wing Me 262. Busemann had predicted at the 1936 Yalta Conference the benefit of swept wings in reducing drag at high subsonic speeds, and this reduction had subsequently been confirmed by tunnel tests in Germany. These tests had also disclosed a tendency to tip-stalling due to the outboard drift of boundary layer air, but there was no general agreement among German designers on how to cure the resulting pitch-up.

It is worth recalling that the Me 262 had only 12° of sweep, which was hardly significant aerodynamically, and that the Me 163 had 23°, which was used primarily to give this tailless aircraft better pitch damping and control. Both had critical Mach Nos of 0.75, and their maximum dive speeds were Mach 0.86 and 0.82 respectively.

With hindsight, German wartime developments did not provide any of the conquerors with a positive guide to wing planform, since many projects aimed at replacing the Me 262 were to be tailless aircraft. Others employed forward-swept wings to avoid tip-stalling. This ambiguity, combined with the very limited thrust of the engines then available, made straight-wing fighters a logical intermediate step in the development of the first really important Soviet jet fighters.

Lavochkin Loses Again

The Yak-15 was much more of a stop-gap effort than the MiG-9, since its tailwheel undercarriage gave a poor field of view when taxying, its metal tailwheel produced a rough ride, and its inclined jet blew debris across the airfield. Nor was its in-flight performance remarkable. The 435 knots (805 km/hr) of the Yak-15 was less than the 453 knots (840 km/hr) of the He 162 *Volksjaeger*, which weighed more than 5940 lb (2700 kg) and had a BMW 003 of only 1760 lb (800 kg) thrust.

The Yak-15 was therefore quickly replaced by the Yak-17, with a tricycle undercarriage, increased internal fuel, and the more powerful 2200 lb (1000 kg) RD-10A engine. Maximum speed increased to 448 knots (830 km/hr), despite a gross weight of 7055 lb (3200 kg) with tip tanks. Reports indicate that over 400 were built, the first entering service in 1948. The production contract had been contested unsuccessfully by the La-152, which had a fuselage-mounted undercarriage. This gave a narrow track, but it later proved useful in making the aircraft more suitable for wing development work.

One result was the La-160, which had a 35° swept wing and matching tailplane, and flew on 24 June 1948. This was the first Soviet swept-wing aircraft, and featured two full-chord wing fences on either side. Wing fences have remained a feature of Soviet combat aircraft until the present day, although they were replaced by dogtooth leading edge extensions in the case of the swing-wing MiG-23/27. The Soviets do not appear to use vortex generators on a significant scale.

The La-160 was only a technology demonstrator, but it was into the air three months ahead of the XP-86 Sabre, which flew on 1 October 1947. It was even further ahead of Europe's first swept-wing fighter, the Saab J29, which flew on 1 September 1948. The La-160 is credited with 567 knots (1050 km/hr) at 18,700 ft (5700 m), corresponding to around Mach 0.92. It had an afterburning RD-10F of 2425 lb (1100 kg) thrust, hence this speed may have been attained in level flight, though it sounds slightly optimistic.

Having rushed into service some very basic jet fighters, the next priority was to obtain some more powerful engines. Suitable powerplants could be developed in-country, given time, but a further stop-gap was highly desirable.

Stalin is reported to have said of this problem: *'Who would be so stupid as to let us have their engines?'*. The answer was duly provided by Britain's Labour Government. Before the end of 1946 the first of 40 Rolls-Royce Derwents and 25 Nenes had arrived in the Soviet Union, where they were quickly distributed to the various fighter and bomber OKBs for prototype installations. Others went to engine design offices, to be taken apart and copied for local unlicensed manufacture.

In due course the Derwent became the 3520 lb (1600 kg) RD-500, while the Nene became the 5000 lb (2270 kg) RD-45. The latter was particularly important, as it provided more than twice the thrust of the more powerful of the ex-German engines, yet it had almost the same weight and a 12 per cent lower SFC. The indications were that Soviet aircraft designers had been working for several months in anticipation of this British delivery, as several Rolls-engined types flew before the end of 1947.

Of these aircraft, the Yak-23 *Flora* was a straightforward derivative of the Yak-17, fattened to accommodate a centrifugal-flow engine. Powered by the RD-500 (Derwent), it had a gross weight of 7385 lb (3350 kg) with tip tanks. Its maximum speed was an unremarkable 494 knots (915 km/hr), but it had an initial climb rate of 6700 ft/min (34 m/sec) and a service ceiling of 48,500 ft (14,800 m). It is believed that it served only briefly with the SAF, though over 300 were built and it certainly equipped several East European services.

A Winner from MiG

In contrast to the ultra-conservative Yak-23, the MiG Bureau's I-310 or Type S was a completely new swept-wing aircraft. Designed to fulfil a March 1946 SAF requirement for a high altitude clear weather interceptor, it appears to have been inspired by German WW2 projects such as the Focke-Wulf Ta-152. The preliminary design of the I-130 (which reportedly began life with a T-tail and RD-10 engine) is officially credited to a Soviet engineer named Savitsky, though at the time it was rumoured that a former Heinkel designer (Guenther) was responsible.

The first prototype flew on 2 July 1947, with a test pilot named Weiss. However, it had dihedral (a fundamental mistake in a swept-wing aircraft), and Weiss was killed shortly afterwards in a landing accident, due to a combination of Dutch Roll and loss of aileron effectiveness at low speeds. The next aircraft, regarded as the true I-130 prototype, flew on 30 December 1947, powered by an RD-45 (Nene) and with Viktor Yuganov at the controls.

The I-310 had a 35° wing with an 11 per cent thickness/chord ratio. The wing was mid-set, giving a clean wing-body junction, though it complicated the engine air supply. The plenum chamber was fed by four ducts, to get air around the cockpit and the wing. One innovative feature of the I-310 was a detachable ventral gunpack with two 23 mm and one 37 mm cannon, firing in close proximity to the intake lip. Like the air duct arrangement, this demonstrated the tolerance of the Nene engine.

Appearing just over two years after the end of the war, the I-310 was a staggering advance over anything the Soviets (or the Germans) had flown before. It won for the two project team leaders the Stalin Prize for 1947, worth 150,000 roubles to each, and in the spring of 1948 it was ordered into production as the MiG-15.

Deliveries began late that year, and reports indicate that around 18,000 of this family were built, to serve with 27 air forces. The first production version was licence-built in Poland as the LIM-1 and in Czechoslovakia as the C-102. The single-seat fighter also provided the basis for a two-seat advanced trainer, the MiG-15UTI

Midget, which was licence built at the LIM-3 and CS-102.

The initial production MiG-15 differed from the prototypes in having anhedral, a slightly lower tailplane, and a shorter jetpipe, requiring more fin sweep to maintain tailplane position. Leading edge slats had been tested on the second I-310 as a means to cure a high speed loss of aileron effectiveness, but these were abandoned in favour of a pair of full-chord fences on either wing. The early series aircraft had a clean gross weight of 10,600 lb (4805 kg), a maximum level speed of Mach 0.91 at 36,000 ft (11,000 m) and a service ceiling of 50,000 ft (15,200 m).

From early 1950 production switched to the

Manufacture of the MiG-15 was undertaken in Czechoslovakia and Poland as the S 102 and LIM-1 respectively, the MiG-15*bis* being designated S 103 and LIM-2. This Soviet-operated aircraft carries light bombs underwing.

MiG-15bis, which had been the subject of a weight reduction programme, and was equipped with the more powerful Klimov VK-1 (Nene derivative). This gave a thrust of 5950 lb (2700 kg) and raised the service ceiling significantly, though the maximum dive speed remained unchanged at Mach 0.92 due to the thick wing. In some (if not all) production aircraft this limit was imposed by automatic airbrake extension. Maximum weight rose to 13,330 lb (6045 kg) with two bombs. The MiG-15bis was licence-built as the LIM-2 in Poland, the S-103 in Czechoslovakia, and the Jaguar in Hungary. Under the Sino-Soviet aid agreement signed in October 1951, it was intended that China should build the MiG-15bis and the VK-1A engine, but in October 1954 this plan was dropped in favour of the MiG-17 and VK-1F.

The MiG-15 flew its first combat mission in Korea on 1 November 1950, when a flight of F-51s was attacked without effect. The US 5th Air Force responded by bringing in the F-86A-5, which carried out its first mission on December

17th. The USAF normally cites an exchange ratio of 10:1 for Korea, on the basis of 792 MiGs destroyed in the air for the loss of 78 Sabres. These figures come from the USAF Statistical Digest for FY53. However, it may be noted that the MiGs also destroyed in the air 43 other aircraft, namely 14 F-80s, 18 F-84s, 10 F-51s and one F-94. In the section listed 'lost due to unknown enemy action', the MiGs probably accounted for the 13 F-86s and 41 other fighters (ie, 16 F-80s, 13 F-84s and 12 F-51s). Of the various 'missing' aircraft, the MiGs presumably accounted for some of the 13 F-86s and 108 other fighters (38 F-80s, 33 F-84s, 32 F-51s, two F-94s and three F-82s). It is also worth bearing in mind that the Sabre pilots generally chose the altitude of the encounter, to ensure superior performance. If it had been a question of Sabres intercepting high-flying MiGs making armed reconnaissance missions, the kill ratio could have been very different.

The MiG-15bis had been introduced in mid-1951, just ahead of the F-86E. The F-86F arrived in June 1952. At the time it was assumed that the MiGs (which operated from airfields in China, to be safe from USAF bombing) were being flown by 'volunteers of the Chinese People's Liberation Army', backed by a few Soviet instructors. However, the postwar USAF assessment (judging by Gen Momyer's book *Air Power in Three Wars*) appears to have been that the MiGs were mainly Soviet squadrons rotating at six-week intervals, though there were also some Chinese and Polish units involved.

Prior to the end of the conflict, the only opportunity to examine a MiG-15 on the ground occurred when a early example, which had been built at Kuibyshev in 1948, ditched off the North Korean coast in July 1951. Though it sank in 17 ft (5.2 m) of water, it was recovered by the Royal Navy, and duly transported to Wright-Patterson AFB for study.

Remaining in Eastern Bloc service long after its single-seat progenitor had been retired, the two-seat MiG-15UTI *Midget* proved to be a sturdy, workmanlike advanced trainer. The second seat was inserted aft of the standard cockpit. (*Philip Handleman*)

In May 1953 Polish pilots defected with two MiG-15bis to the Danish island of Bornholm in the Baltic, where detailed inspections were made by NATO intelligence officers before the aircraft were returned to Poland. However, this was only two months before the end of the Korean War, and the information came too late to have any effect on the fighting.

Meanwhile the 5th Air Force had for some time been dropping leaflets over North Korea, offering $100,000 to any MiG pilot who would deliver his aircraft to Kimpo AB in the south. On 21 September 1953, two months after the end of the conflict, Lt Ro Kum-Suk landed his MiG-15bis at Kimpo and became the instant beneficiary of *'Project Moolah'*.

As tested at WPAFB, this MiG-15bis had a clean take-off weight of 11,070 lb (5020 kg) with 310 Imp gal (1400 litres) of internal fuel, and 40 rounds of 37 mm and 160 of 23 mm ammunition. It was thus much lighter than all the Sabres it encountered, from the early 13,790 lb (6255 kg) F-86A-5 to the ultimate 14,980 lb (6800 kg) F-86F-30.

The MiG-15bis was found to have an initial climb rate of 10,000 ft/min (51.3 m/sec), taking it to 30,000 ft (9150 m) in 4.0 minutes, compared to 8.8 minutes for the F-86E. It had an absolute ceiling of 51,500 ft (15,700 m), which was 3500 ft (1070 m) higher than that of the F-86E.

Maximum level speed was measured as Mach 0.877 at sea level, rising to Mach 0.91 at 35,000 ft (10,700 m). Above this height it was faster than the F-86A-5 and F-86E-5, roughly equal with the slatted F-86F-10, and measurably inferior only to the F-86F-30 with the extended ('6–3') leading edge. It was found that buffeting began at Mach 0.91, with a strong nose-up tendency at Mach 0.93.

The MiG-15bis was rated by USAF evaluation pilots as a good interceptor, excelling in airfield performance, acceleration, climb rate and ceiling, but inferior to the F-86 series (which had a genuine transonic dive performance) as an air superiority fighter. However, an average MiG kill took 1024 rounds of 12.7 mm ammunition, hence it could be said that the Sabre was not very effectively armed.

The MiG's best defensive tactic was a climbing turn. It was found to have a basically good turning performance, but this could not be exploited fully because of its slow rate of roll and the need to avoid spins, of which there was no proper warning. High Mach handling was characterized by loss of control and poor lateral-directional stability. The MiG was felt to be badly equipped, with no radar ranging (though Momyer states that most Sabre pilots got their kills with a fixed sight setting from the 6 o'clock position), no IFF, no anti-G suit provisions, and no parking brake. It also had no gun heating, and was thus prone to stoppages at altitude.

In engineering terms the MiG-15 airframe was basically conventional, although a 60 lb (27.3 kg) anti-flutter weight was located in either outboard leading edge. The tailplane was fixed in flight, but its incidence could be changed on the ground. The elevators and rudders were operated manually, but the ailerons were hydraulically powered, with internal mass balances and aerodynamic sealing to allow manual reversion. All the internal fuel was carried in the fuselage, but the aircraft could carry two 65 Imp gal (295 litre) drop tanks.

A mechanical indication of undercarriage position was provided by red-and-white striped spigots (known as 'soldiers'), projecting through the upper surface of the front fuselage and wings. In emergency the undercarriage could be blown down by compressed air, the air bottles for the main gears being built into the upper legs. The wheelbrakes were pneumatically operated from an air bottle, which was recharged between flights.

A four-man team could change an engine in 60 minutes, although this involved removing the rear fuselage. The team could change a wing in 25 minutes. The gunpack (unlike that of the Hunter, which was replaced by a loaded one) was replenished by lowering it to the ground on four built-in cables and reloading it under the aircraft.

The ejection seat was of very simple design, with no stabilising drogue, no leg restraint, and no protection for the pilot's face. To eject he placed his feet on rests, grasped firing handles in the armrests, jettisoned the canopy with his left hand, and fired the seat with the right. Three seconds after ejection the straps were released automatically, so that the pilot could fall clear and open his parachute.

The mass flow of the cabin conditioning system was felt to be inadequate for hot climates, a shortcoming that remained with the MiG series for many years. The instrument layout was conventional, but simplified to some extent by the use of combined instruments. For example, the normal ASI was combined with a TAS display. Another instrument combined fuel and oil pressures with oil temperature. Weapon-aiming relied on a simple GGS, probably derived from a wartime British design, and with a maximum range setting of 2650 ft (800 m).

Fantail was the NATO reporting name for the Lavochkin La-15, an early operational jet that was overshadowed by the publicity attracted by the MiG-15. *Fantail* operated in the ground-attack role.

Losers and Successors

There had been two RD-45/Nene-engined alternatives to the MiG-15, the high-wing La-168, which first flew on 22 April 1948, and the Yak-30, which looked rather like a Mystere IVA, and flew on 4 September 1948. However, they came on the scene too late, and offered no performance advantage.

Lavochkin then scaled down his design to suit the less powerful RD-500/Derwent, producing the La-174D. Its clean gross of only 8175 lb (3708 kg) made it significantly lighter than the MiG-15, and it offered almost as much performance, though its armament was limited to two 23 mm cannon. It was ordered into series production as the La-15 (*Fantail*), and around 500 were built, though reports suggest it was relegated to the close support role. The La-15 was probably the lightest postwar jet fighter to see large-scale production.

Another Lavochkin development was the La-176, essentially the larger La-168 with a 45°,

9.5 per cent thick wing. It first flew during September 1948, and exceeded the speed of sound in a dive on 26 December 1948, becoming the first Soviet aircraft to do this. For comparison, the F-86A exceeded Mach 1.0 on 26 April 1948 (it is claimed), though 'Chuck' Yeager had already gone supersonic in a climb in the Bell X-1 on 14 October 1947.

Another Soviet aircraft that failed to reach production was the Yak-50, which first flew on 15 July 1949. It had a 45° wing, but was historically noteworthy as probably the first application of a zero-track tricycle undercarriage. This concept was to reappear on several later Yakovlev designs, and on Britain's P.1127/Harrier series, in which it was used to move the mainwheels away from the hot jets during V/STOL.

Both the La-176 and Yak-50 offered performance advantages over the MiG-15, but in seeking a transonic replacement for the SAF's first swept-wing fighter, there were clear advantages in developing that aircraft further, rather than switching to a completely new design.

The MiG bureau's offering was the I-330 or Type SI. Sweep angle was increased to 45°, though on the outer wing it was restricted to 42°, and a third fence was added. Thickness/chord ratio was reduced, but only to 10 per cent. This was thicker than the sections used by MiG's competitors, perhaps because the main undercarriage of the I-330 was wing-mounted. The tips were rounded, the rear fuselage extended, the tailplane span was increased (though its incidence remained fixed in flight), and the airbrakes were revised, probably to increase effectiveness and reduce pitch trim change.

The first I-330 had its maiden flight on 13 January 1950, but was destroyed two months later, reportedly in a high-Mach dive. The second prototype flew a few months later, and the type was ordered into production as the MiG-17. Deliveries began in October 1952, but it did not see service in Korea, where the conflict continued until 27 July 1953. The final clash between MiG-15s and F-86s occurred on July 22nd, when one MiG was destroyed without loss.

The initial production MiG-17 was designated *Fresco A* under the ASCC reporting system, and was a clear weather fighter with the same VK-1 engine as the MiG-15bis. The principal production series was the MiG-17F *Fresco C*, which was licence-built in China as the J-5 and in Poland as the LIM-5. Soviet-built aircraft in Czech service were designated S-104. The MiG-17F is still flying in some numbers in the Third World. It is powered by an afterburning VK-1F of 7500 lb (3400 kg) thrust, and has an empty weight of 8665 lb (3930 kg), a maximum loaded weight of 13,400 lb (6075 kg), and the remarkable service ceiling of 54,500 ft (16,600 m).

The MiG-17PF *Fresco D* was a radar-equipped night fighter with a limited bad-weather capability. It retained the VK-1F engine, but had an *Izumrud* (Emerald) radar with its search antenna in an acorn fairing in the middle of the intake, and a ranging antenna in an enlarged upper intake lip. The 37 mm cannon was deleted in favour of a third 23 mm. The MiG-17PFU *Fresco E* was a night fighter with provisions for four AA-1 *Alkali* bean-riding air-to-air missiles, and with the guns deleted.

It is believed that around 6000 MiG-17s were built in the Soviet Union, plus 1000 in Poland and more than 2000 in China, where the first Shenyang-built aircraft flew in 1956. Recently published information on Chinese production includes the fact that 767 J-5s had been completed by the end of 1959, and 1061 two-seat JJ-5s by the end of 1986. The JJ-5 was a Shenyang development, which first flew on 8 May 1966, and used the front and centre fuselage sections from the MiG-15UTI. The VK-1F engine was manufactured as the WP-5. It has been reported that over 100 two-seaters were exported from Shenyang under the designation FT-5. In total the MiG-17 series has been operated by around 30 nations, making it probably the world's most widely-used jet fighter.

Though it lacked the refinement of some contemporary Western fighters, the MiG-17F was in its day a very practical lightweight short-range fighter-bomber, directly comparable to the Hunter, which entered service one year later. The Iraqi Air Force has operated both types, and concluded that the MiG-17F made a somewhat better high altitude interceptor due to its afterburner, but that the larger Hunter was better for

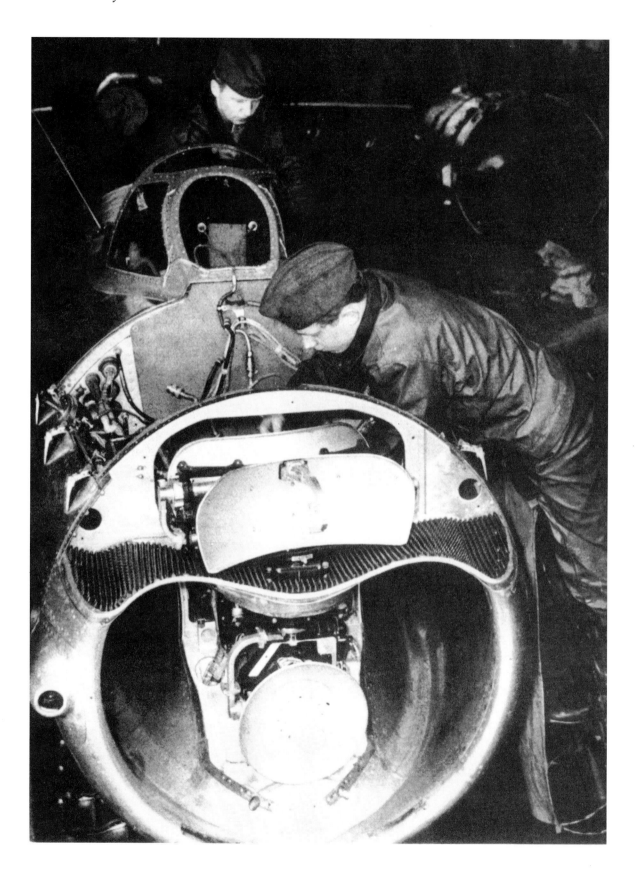

ground attack. In a dogfight they were felt to be evenly matched, despite the fixed tailplane of the MiG. The lateral handling of the MiG-17 is better than for the MiG-15, but is far from perfect. In one well-known incident, the pilot of an Indonesian MiG-17 attempted a low level rolling pullout during a flying display, and snap-rolled straight into the ground.

The MiG-17 has seen operational service in many parts of the world. During the Suez crisis of 1956 the availability of Czech-built MiG-17s to defend Egyptian airfields restricted RAF bombing to the hours of darkness. In the period July–October 1958 PLAAF F-5s fought several battles with Nationalist Chinese F-86s over the offshore islands Kinmen and Matsu in the Taiwan Strait, and the Nationalists claimed the destruction of 31 F-5s for the loss of only two Sabres. In subsequent years the MiG-17 was often employed in shooting wars, most notably during

Arab attacks on Israel and in the defence of North Vietnamese targets against US aircraft. Half the NVNAF fighters shot down were MiG-17s, ie, 92 out of 184.

Through The Barrier

In the autumn of 1950 an OR was issued by the SAF for a day fighter that could achieve supersonic speed in level flight. To make this possible, it was felt that thinner and more highly swept wings would be required, and more powerful axial-flow engines.

In this case there were two unsuccessful contenders. The La-190 had a Lyulka AL-5, a 55° wing that was 6.1 per cent thick and mid-set (presumably bolted to ring-frames), a high tailplane and a zero-track tricycle undercarriage. It

Maintenance at a Warsaw Pact MiG-17 base in the late-Fifties. The aircraft is a PF variant which had a limited all-weather intercept capability. The RP-5 *Izumrud* radar comprised fixed scan in the top intake lip and conical scan in the lower inlet splitter. On the left is the combat camera housing.

North American flew the prototype YF-100A just four months ahead of Mikoyan's I-350(M) which later became the MiG-19 *Farmer*. Somehow, the Super Sabre epitomized those early days of supersonic flight. The USAF Skyblazers flew the type in the mid-sixties.

East Germany, like other users of the type, operated
the MiG-19PM which discarded the cannon in favour
of an all-missile armament of four *Alkali* (AA-1). *Scan
Odd* X-band radar gave the aircraft a limited
all-weather capability.

reportedly attained Mach 1.03 in level flight on
11 March 1951. The Yak-1000 was broadly
similar, but had a cropped-delta planform. It is
believed that this aircraft suffered an accident
during high-speed taxying trials, and never flew.

Once again the MiG bureau won the contest.
Although it had its share of early development
problems, the resulting MiG-19 Farmer stood
alongside the F-100 Super Sabre as the world's
first production fighters capable of supersonic
speed in level flight. It was also to provide the
basis for the Nanchang J-6, which has been
China's principal fighter for decades, and in turn
served as the basis for the Q-5 *Fantan* attack
aircraft.

Firm details of the early history of the MiG-19
will have to wait for the official bureau history to
be published. The first prototype, the I-350, is
believed to have had a single AL-5 engine and a
T-tail, and to have flown by October 1951. The
I-360 was extensively redesigned to accommodate two Mikulin AM-5s, but it crashed, due to
tailplane flutter. The I-370 is said to have had two
VK-7F engines.

The definitive prototype was the I-350(M),
which took an important step forward with a
fuselage-mounted tailplane, though this remained (unlike that of the F-100) above the wing-
plane. The maiden flight took place on 18
September 1953, only slightly behind the
YF-100A, which had flown on May 25th.

Pre-series deliveries of the MiG-19F began in
December 1953, at which stage the programme
was running slightly ahead of the F-100A. It was
powered by two Tumansky AM-5F engines, each
giving a thrust of 6700 lb (3040 kg). It had a 58°
leading edge, and an 8.24 per cent section,
compared to the 45°, 6.0 per cent wing of the
F-100. The MiG-19F avoided tip-stalling by
means of a very deep fence on either wing, rather
than the automatic leading edge slats of the Super
Sabre.

Underside view of a MiG-19 *Farmer* showing the 58°
wing sweepback, two 23 mm NR-23 cannon in the
wingroots and the slab all-flying tailplanes.

As in the case of the MiG-17, a night fighter version (MiG-19PF) was developed with the *Izumrud* radar. Both the MiG-19F and -19PF reportedly suffered severe control problems in transonic flight, probably because they lacked the hydraulically-powered flying tail that US fighters had used since the F-86E. The introduction of a slab 'flying' tailplane produced the MiG-19S day fighter, which also had Tumansky RD-9s of 7165 lb (3250 kg) and a ventral airbrake in addition to two lateral units. Deliveries began in 1955, in which year a total of 48 MiG-19s (a

Cockpit of the Nanchang A-5K modernized with French equipment with Thomson-CSF acting as prime contractor.
(*Thomson-CSF*)

mix of subtypes) appeared at Tushino.

In the following year the original mix of two 23 mm and one 37 mm cannon was replaced by three 30 mm, two of which were mounted in the wingroots. This new gun arrangement was probably necessitated by the surge tendency of axial-flow engines. The MiG-19P combined the slab tail with *Izumrud* radar, and the MiG-19PM mounted AA-1 *Alkali* missiles in place of cannon.

It is believed that around 2000 MiG-19s were constructed in the Soviet Union before production was transferred to Czechoslovakia in the late 1950s. At Shenyang, efforts to assemble and later build the MiG-19 as the J-6 began in 1958, but quality control was unsatisfactory, and production deliveries began only at the end of 1963. The first locally-assembled MiG-19P flew on 17 December 1958, and the first MiG-19S on 30 September 1959. The Nanchang facility also

The Chinese produced an attack version of the MiG-19 known as the Nachang Q-5. This differed externally mainly in having lateral intakes and a nose probably intended for radar, although this was subsequently not fitted.
(*Roy Braybrook*)

manufactured the MiG-19P and -19PM, the AA-1 missile being built as the PL-1 and the RD-9 engine as the WP-6. The RP-5 *Izumrud* radar was also built in China.

Published information for a late-production MiG-19S includes an empty weight of 12,700 lb (5760 kg), which is similar to that for a Harrier GR.3 without guns. Maximum weight is given as 20,065 lb (9100 kg). It has a maximum speed of Mach 1.36, an initial climb rate of 22,650 ft/min (115 m/sec), and a service ceiling of 58,700 ft (17,900 m).

The most significant derivative of the MiG-19 series is the Nanchang Q-5 attack aircraft, which was launched as a project in August 1958. However, it then suffered a series of delays, and the first flight eventually took place on 4 June 1965. Modifications were then introduced, and two further aircraft flew in October 1969. China is now thought to have 400–500 Q-5s in service, in addition to over 2500 J-6s.

The original idea in developing the Q-5 appears to have been to use lateral intakes to free the nose for radar, while rearranging the aircraft interior to make space for a ventral weapons bay. This may have been planned to give a higher penetration speed or to avoid kinetic heating of a nuclear weapon. In any event, the radar was never fitted, and the bay appears to be permanently closed and used to house extra fuel tanks, which give the Q-5 some 70 per cent more internal fuel than the J-6. Four weapons pylons are mounted under the fuselage, and four under either wing, although two of these are so close that it is impossible to use them simultaneously.

Initial production took the form of three principal variants: the Q-5 I, Q-5 II and Q-5 III, which for export became the A-5 I etc. At least 160 A-5s have been supplied to Pakistan, 40 to North Korea, and 20 have been ordered Bangladesh. Pakistan uses the A-5 III (in addition to the F-6 and FT-6), with Martin-Baker PKD-10 zero-zero seats and provisions for the Matra Magic AAM. Reports suggest that around 100 torpedo-carrying Q-5s were built for the Chinese Navy.

A flight-refuellable version of the Q-5 was projected in the mid-1980s, and in 1986 an MoU was signed by CATIC and Flight Refuelling Ltd on a programme to convert Xian H-6 bombers (Tu-16s) to tankers for the Q-5. Contract negotiations were proceeding when the project was stopped by COCOM at the request of the Japanese, who evidently felt that a flight-refuelled Q-5 might pose a threat. However, China is still looking for a tanker (using either the H-6 or the Y-8 *Cub* transport) for the Q-5 and F-7 series.

In order to extend the life of the A-5 programme, CATIC has entered into agreements with two European companies to develop jointly improved variants with modern cockpits and Western nav-attack and communications systems. The A-5K *Kong Yun* (Cloud) is being developed with Thomson-CSF, and the first prototype (serial 21092) had its maiden flight on 7 September 1988. In 1990 the French Defence Minister announced the termination of the A-5K programme by the Chinese government. The first of two A-5Ms being developed with Aeritalia flew on 30 August 1988, but crashed two months later on October 17th, reportedly due to pilot error.

The A-5M is equipped with two uprated 8270 lb (3750 kg) Wopen WP-6A turbojets. It has an empty weight of 14,630 lb (6634 kg) and a maximum take-off weight of 26,460 lb (12,000 kg). Maximum speed is Mach 1.2, compared to Mach 1.12 for the A-5 III, and 'actual' (presumably service) ceiling is given as 52,500 ft (16,000 m). With a 4410 lb (2000 kg) external bombload, the A-5M has a LO-LO radius of more than 160 nm (300 Km), and HI-LO-LO-HI radius of more than 215 nm (400 km).

The importance of the J-6 and Q-5 series for the PLAAF is illustrated by reports that of the 948 aircraft deployed along the border with Vietnam during the 'punitive war' of February–March 1979, some 580 were J-6s and 120 were Q-5s. The remainder consisted of 98 J-5s, 28 J-7s (MiG-21s), 94 H-5s (Il-28s) and 24 H-6s (Tu-16s). However, the PLAAF aircraft took little part in the conflict, since Vietnam had highly effective SAMs and AAA, and far superior MiG-21s. Air defence for PLA units in Vietnam was left to the 50 km SA-2, and no ground attack missions were flown, although the border was crossed in approximately 660 sorties. Casualties among PLA ground forces were consequently heavy: around 30,000 out of the 250,000 men involved.

Defence By Night

The development of the first Soviet jet-powered day fighters and their Chinese derivatives has been considered in some detail, since at that time the day fighter represented the cutting-edge of aviation technology. However, the advent of the nuclear bomber put the emphasis firmly on interception (rather than air superiority), and this mission clearly had to be carried out at night as well as by day. Soviet efforts to produce an effective day/night all-weather interceptor began in 1947, although this programme was to come to fruition only in the mid-1950s.

The first series of projects was based in the use of swept wings and a pair of Nene-derivatives, RD-45Fs or VK-1s, to maintain a reasonable performance despite the weight of radar and the extra fuel needed, compared to a short daylight

TOP RIGHT **Dating from the early-fifties, the Yak-25** *Flashlight* **was the Soviet Air Force's first production jet-powered night fighter. The large nose radome enclosed a** *Scan Three* **intercept radar and under the fuselage were two 37 mm cannon.**

RIGHT **Behind the strongly-framed 57 mm thick windscreen, the two crew members of the Yak-25 enjoyed the use of much-improved ejection seats and operated in a pressurized and heated cockpit. The canopy was rearward-sliding.**

intercept. In view of the large diameter of these engines, the obvious approach might have been to hang them on the wings (Meteor-style), but all three design teams chose to place them in tandem in the fuselage. The MiG bureau's I-320 (Type R) and the La-200 had two crew members side-by-side between the engines, while the single-seat Su-15 (Type P) placed the pilot in the nose. The Su-15 first flew on 11 January 1949, the La-200 on 9 September 1949, and the I-320 on an unpublished date in 1950. All had the *Izumrud* radar and 37 mm cannon: two in the case of the Su-15 and three each for the two-seaters. None got beyond the prototype stage, probably because of poor performance and the fact that this small radar could be mounted in aircraft such as the MiG-17 and -19.

The first production Soviet jet night fighter was the Yak-25 *Flashlight*. It was a tandem-seater with a mid-set 45° wing and two underslung axial-flow engines, 5735 lb (2600 kg) non-afterburning versions of the RD-9 used in the MiG-19. This arrangement left the nose free for a large radar, known to NATO as *Scan Three*. It had a zero-track tricycle undercarriage, and two 37 mm guns mounted under the front fuselage. It is believed that the Yak-25 first flew in 1952/53, and that around 1000 had been built by 1958, when production ended.

The Yak-25 appears to have been somewhat larger and better powered than the Meteor NF series, with a normal take-off weight of around 20,000 lb (9000 kg) and a maximum speed of 590 knots (1090 km/hr). It was officially stated to have a ceiling of 45,600 ft (13,900 m) and a range of 1600 nm (3000 km). This figure implies an unusually large fuel fraction, but most of the centre fuselage was available for tankage. Wing area was 302 sq ft (28 m²).

Although aesthetically unattractive, the Yak-25 did provide a basis for further developments in both the air defence and tactical reconnaissance roles. For these derivative designs, afterburners were introduced, and the wing planform was improved by means of leading edge extensions.

Jet Bombers

It may be assumed that in the immediate postwar period the Soviets gave the development of jet bombers a lower priority than fighters, since they had no atomic bomb, and no short-term prospect of producing a jet bomber that could reach US targets. In the short term, the SAF would have to rely on piston-engined bombers, notably the Tu-4 *Bull*, which had been copied from B-29s that had landed at Vladivostock in 1944, after attacking Japanese targets.

The principal contestants for bomber orders were the Tupolev and Ilyushin bureas. Tupolev had a much larger team, and as first into the air with the Type 77, a twin-Nene derivative of the piston-engined Tu-2 *Bat*. The Type 77 flew on 27 June 1947, but was underpowered, and was quickly followed by the three-engined Types 73 and 78. In either case a Derwent or RD-500 was added in the rear fuselage, fed by a dorsal intake in the fashion of the 727 or Trident centreline inlet. A swept tailplane maintained pitch control at high speeds.

The unconventional three-engined arrangement was greeted with something short of enthusiasm, and development switched to the use of two of the more powerful VK-1s, which also left the rear fuselage free for a tail turret. Several hundred Type 81s were built for Soviet Naval Aviation as the Tu-14 *Bosun*, with deliveries beginning at the end of 1949.

The Tupolev bureau also produced the first Soviet swept-wing bomber, the Type 82, which was powered by two VK-1s and flew in February 1949. However, no production order was forthcoming, and this OKB left the tactical bomber field to concentrate on strategic bombers and commercial transports.

With less assets at its disposal, the Ilyushin OKB was slower to get a successful jet bomber flying, but eventually won the contest for tactical bomber orders. Starting from scratch, and appreciating how little thrust was available, the bureau began with a four-engined design, the Il-22. This looked like a small jet-powered cousin of the B-29, with a shoulder-set wing carrying four Lyulka TR-1 engines on short pylons. Surprisingly, it flew on 24 July 1947, only one month

The Ilyushin Il-28 *Beagle* can claim to be the Soviet Union's first production jet bomber. This picture of a Czech-operated example clearly show the Il-K6 tail turret containing twin 23 mm cannon, a defensive position which was a hallmark of most Soviet bombers of the period and reflected World War 2 thinking.

after the Tupolev 77 jet derivative of the Tu-2. However, the Il-22 reportedly made only a few flights, possibly because of problems associated with its narrow (fuselage-mounted) under-carriage. It was to have been followed by the Il-24 with four RD-500s and main undercarriage units moved to wing-mounted pods (a feature of many subsequent Tupolev designs), but this project was never built.

The only other Soviet four-jet bomber of the period was the Su-10, a somewhat heavier air-craft with TR-1As mounted in vertical pairs at mid-span, reminiscent of the Shorts Sperrin. The Su-10 never flew, and the programme was termi-nated in 1948.

The availability of the more powerful Rolls-Royce engines transformed the prospects for Soviet jet bombers, just as they had done for fighters. Abandoning its four-engined series of light bomber projects, the Ilyushin OKB pro-duced the Il-28 *Beagle*. It first flew on 8 July 1948, and (having won against the somewhat heavier three-engined Tupolev 78) entered ser-vice in September 1950, replacing the Tu-2 *Bat*. The Il-28 was the first Soviet jet bomber to be produced in large numbers (around 3000), and it was exported to many countries. Variants in-cluded the Il-28U *Mascot*, and a target-towing aircraft used until recently by the Finnish Air Force.

A number of Il-28s were sold to China, where the Harbin factory was allowed to repair these aircraft and manufacture high-usage replacement parts. Starting with the repair drawings, the Harbin facility launched in 1963 a reverse-engineering programme, which led to a Chinese copy (the H-5) making its first flight on 25 September 1966. Production was launched in April 1967, and around 1500 were built, includ-ing some 186 HJ-5 trainers.

Although the Il-28 lacks the speed and high altitude performance of Britain's Canberra, which first flew one year later (13 May 1949), the Ilyushin may be more useful in a COIN war, due to its surface-mapping radar, two fixed 23 mm guns in the front fuselage, and a twin 23 mm

A posed picture of an AV-MF Il-28T version of the *Beagle* with one of the two 533 mm torpedoes which it carried in a modified weapons bay. (*TASS*)

turret in the tail. The Il-28 achieved fame in 1962, when, along with SS-3 *Shyster* missiles, some 42 were supplied to Castro's Cuba, threatening the southern US. The American Administration made it clear that this situation could not be tolerated, and two months after their arrival these aircraft were shipped out.

The Il-28 has a high-set straight 12 per cent wing, and swept tail surfaces, though the tailplane incidence is fixed. Nene engines were used for the prototype, but the production aircraft has 5950 lb (2700 kg) VK-1As. The main undercarriage units are mounted on the undersides of the nacelles, the wheels turning to lie flat below the engines when retracted.

Empty weight is 28,450 lb (12,900 kg), and normal take-off weight is 40,600 lb (18,400 kg). A Czech source credits the Il-28 with a maximum speed of 505 knots (935 km/hr) and a ceiling of 41,000 ft (12,500 m). At the time of the Cuban deployment, the CIA gave it a radius of 800 nm (1480 km).

The Medium Bomber

Whereas the West designed its medium bombers on the basis of multiple off-the-shelf engines (as illustrated by Britain's four-engined Victor and Valiant, and America's six-engined B-47), the Soviet Union developed for this application a new engine series in the 10-ton class. The first aircraft to use these engines was the swept-wing Tu-16 *Badger*, powered initially by two Mikulin AM-3 turbojets of 18,000 lb (8200 kg) thrust. In the course of its long life, this rating has been raised gradually to 21,000 lb (9500 kg) with the AM-3M.

The use of only two engines makes possible a relatively clean installation. The AM-3s are buried in the wing roots, and the nacelles are area-ruled to give the highest possible drag-rise Mach No. In achieving high speed, the Tu-16

may benefit from the housings for the four-wheel main bogeys, which retract into trailing edge fairings. These may function aerodynamically like the Karman fairings of the Convair 990.

Although a completely new design, the Tu-16 was influenced by the Tu-4 in terms of defensive

armament: it has three twin-23 mm remotely-controlled barbettes, in addition to its fixed forward-firing 23 mm cannon (which is deleted for those variants with the large nose radome).

Clearly designed as a bomber for the European theatre, the Tu-16 first flew in 1952, and it remained in production throughout much of that decade. Nine aircraft took part in the 1954 May Day flypast, suggesting that the first squadron may have been operational by the following year with Strategic Aviation.

The basic *Badger A* has a glazed nose, a small

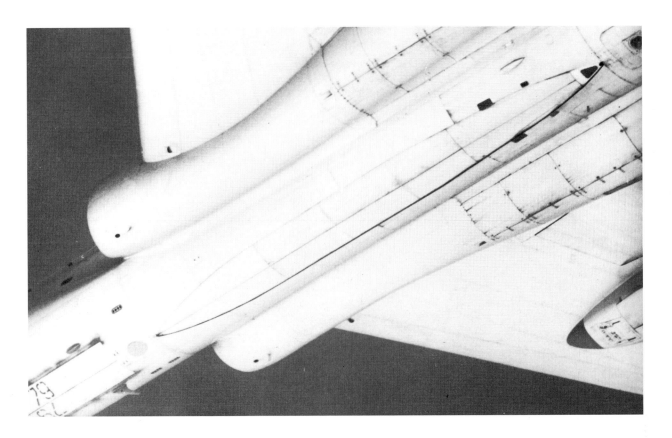

At the Monino Museum, Moscow, is this Tu-16 which could be a prototype or early development airframe for the series. Production of all *Badgers* ran to more than 2000 of which some 300 continue in service.

chin radome, and free-fall bombs. It is now employed primarily as a tanker, using tip-to-tip refuelling (a unique Soviet development) for other Tu-16s, or a drogue to refuel probe-equipped Tu-22 *Blinders*.

The next variant to be seen was *Badger B*, with provisions for two AS-1 *Kennel* anti-ship missiles under the wings. *Badger C* has a radar nose and can carry a single AS-2 *Kipper* under the centre fuselage. A later sub-series (*Badger C-Mod*) re-

TOP LEFT To accommodate the large AS-2 *Kipper* anti-ship missile, the Tu-16 *Badger C* had its bomb-bay doors modified to carry the weapon in a semi-recessed position. Large access panels under the rear of the engine trunking allow maintenance and removal of the Mikulin RD-3Ms.

LEFT The Il-54 *Blowlamp* was first seen at Kubinka in 1956, and was clearly a possible Il-28 replacement. The bicycle undercarriage was still innovative at the time.

tains this AS-2 capability, but can alternatively carry two A-S-6 *Kingfish* missiles under the wings. *Badger D* has a radar nose, but is dedicated to maritime reconnaissance and ELINT duties, and is distinguished by three small ventral radomes. *Badger E* and *F* are ELINT aircraft that are also used for photo-reconnaissance missions. The *E* has two small ventral radomes, and the *F* has two underwing electronics packs.

Some *Badger Bs* have been converted to *Gs*, with provisions for two AS-5 *Kelt* rocket-powered missiles. The *Badger G-Mod* can alternatively carry two AS-6s. *Badger H* is a glazed-nose electronics warfare aircraft with a limited jamming capability and the ability to lay chaff corridors. *Badger J* is a more capable jamming version, with an ECM gondola under the centre fuselage. *Badger K* is the latest glazed-nose ELINT variant.

Of around 2000 Tu-16s built, it is thought that about 400 are still flown by Strategic Aviation, plus 300 by Naval Aviation. Small numbers were exported to Egypt, Indonesia, Iraq and Libya. The Tu-16 has been used operationally by Egypt (launching missiles against Israel), and by Iraq.

In September 1957 the Soviet government granted a licence for the Tu-16 to be built in China at Harbin and Xian as the H-6. The first locally-assembled H-6 flew at Harbin on 27 September 1959, but in 1961 the programme was transferred to Xian, where the first Chinese-built aircraft (designated H-6A) had its maiden flight

'Give me the hose and probe anyday', might be one pilot's comment on the unique wingtip to wingtip flight refuelling system used by Tu-16s. The right-hand aircraft in this duo is the tanker and just visible is the hose extending between the two.

RIGHT The three main views depict the *Badger F* Elint version of the Tu-16, with the additional side-view of the *Badger D* maritime reconnaissance/Elint variant. (*Pilot Press*)

BOTTOM RIGHT *Badger* continues in use for a variety of roles, mainly with the AV-MF. Tupolev thoughtfully stowed the large four-wheel main bogies in streamlined pods, shown to advantage in this view of a *Badger C*.

on 24 December 1968. This type served as a platform for some of the nuclear bomb tests at Lop Nur, and the locally-developed H-6D (first flight 29 August 1981) has provisions for two C-601 anti-ship missiles.

Chinese data for the B-6D includes a 20,944 lb (9500 kg) rating for its Wopen-8 engines, an empty weight of 84,950 lb (38,530 kg), and a maximum take-off weight of 167,100 lb (75,800 kg). Service ceiling is given as 39,360 ft (12,0000 m), maximum cruise speed is 424 knots (786 km/hr), and radius of action is 970 nm (1800 km). Ferry range is 2320 nm (4300 km), and maximum endurance is 5 hr 40 min.

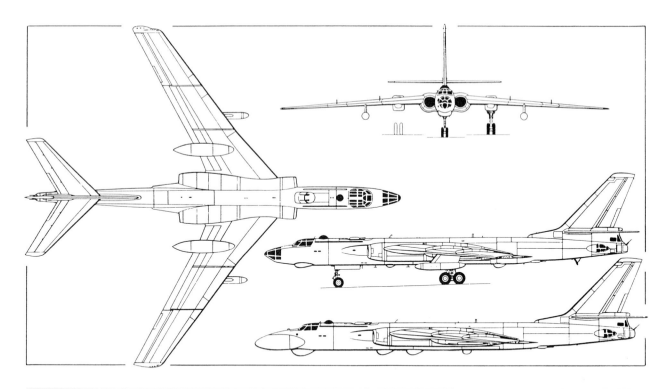

The Strategic Bomber

The availability of the massive AM-3 engine encouraged the development of a heavy four-jet bomber with (flight-refuelled) potential for attacks of North America. The OR is believed to have been issued in 1949, though the resulting Myasishchev M-4 did not fly until 1953. Broadly comparable in weight and performance to an early model B-52, the M-4 has swept wings and tail surfaces, engines buried in the wing roots in what was then the British fashion, and a Boeing-style bicycle undercarriage with tip-mounted outriggers. The original model (*Bison A*) had four twin-23 mm barbettes and (in some cases) a fixed nose gun. It is believed to have entered service in 1956, though this version was soon converted to the tanker role, probably because its radius was totally inadequate for the strategic bombing task.

Bison B appears to have been a major improvement, with vastly more powerful 28,660 lb (13,000 kg) Soloviev D-15 engines. Gun armament was reduced to three barbettes, and this type seems to have been used by Naval Aviation for maritime reconnaissance. It first flew in 1957, and two years later (under the designation 201-M) established a number of speed and load-to-height records. These included a 1000 km closed circuit speed of 555 knots (1028 km/hr), while carrying a 59,535 lb (27,000 kg) load. *Bison C* is a modified version with an enlarged nose radar.

The M-4 is believed to have an empty weight of around 200,000 lb (90,000 kg) and a normal take-off weight of approximately 365,000 lb (165,000 kg). It has a radius of about 3000 nm (5600 km). Some (if not all) M-4s have been scrapped (literally cut in two) under the SALT-II Treaty.

If the M-4 fell short of its design objective as a strategic bomber, its place was taken by the Tu-95 *Bear*, one of the most remarkable aircraft produced in the Soviet Union. The Tu-95 is absolutely unique in combining swept wings with unducted propellers, though the present-day development of propfan engines may lead to other production aircraft fitting this description.

In the 1950s the general Western view was certainly that the combination was illogical, since

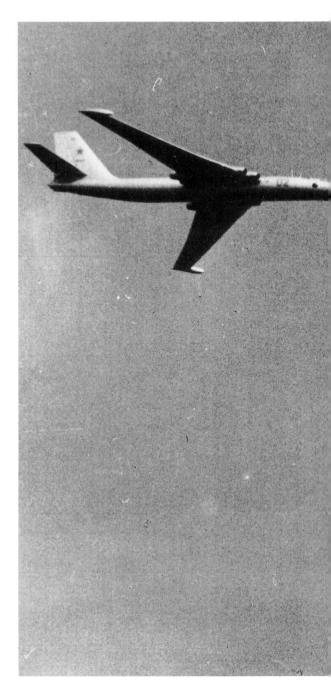

ABOVE Designed at the behest of Stalin, the Myasishchev M-4 was the first Soviet four-jet long-range bomber capable of reaching North America. *Bison A*s are shown during a 1950s flypast over Moscow.

RIGHT *Bison B* had increased sensors for the reconnaissance role and incorporated a refuelling probe in the nose. A number of *Bisons* carried this horizontally-split colour scheme, the lighter shade presumably acting as an anti-flash finish.

the swept wing and the propeller are suited to quite different speed brackets. However, Tupolev was aiming to combine extremely long range, which (in the absence of high-bypass turbofans) demanded the propulsive efficiency of propellers, with a high dash speed over the target, which required a swept wing.

The programme began around 1950, when a German team, led by Dr Ferdinand Brandner and associated with the Kuznetsov engine bureau, began work on the 12,000 shp powerplant that eventuated as the NK-12. The design aim was to achieve a maximum speed of Mach 0.85 at 36,000 ft (11,000 m), with propellers turning at 750 rpm, corresponding (they calculated) to a tip

---

Bear E version of the Tu-95 over solid cloud cover. Initially under-estimated by the West, this most famous of all Soviet 'bombers' remains the symbol of Socialist power projection with a service life expected to extend to the end of the nineties.

---

speed of Mach 1.13. Despite the use of eight-blade contra-rotating propellers to absorb the power in the smallest possible diameter, the tips would thus still be supersonic at the design dash speed.

The long-range cruise speed of the Tu-95 is considerably slower than its maximum. It is normally encountered on patrol at around Mach 0.67 at 36,000 ft (11,000 m). American intelligence sources have credited it with a true maximum speed of Mach 0.80, and a radius of 3450 nm (6400 km). With a reduced payload, the series is known to be capable of operating between Moscow and Havana nonstop and unrefuelled, a distance of 5830 nm (10,800 km).

The *Bear* series is thought to have been in continuous low-rate production for about 35 years, though the designation was changed to Tu-142 from 1973, due to significant airframe modifications. Something in the region of 400 have probably been built, although only around 150 remain with Strategic Aviation and 80 (mainly *Bear F*s) with Naval Aviation.

Boeing's equivalent to the Tu-95 series was the B-52, but instead of using large turboprops, the American designers opted for eight podded jets to get the performance. This sombre example is a B-52G. (*Barry Wheeler*)

The original glazed-nose *Bear A* strategic bomber first flew in late 1954, and it entered service in early 1956. It had a small chin radome and three twin-23 mm turrets. However, by the late 1950s the role of the strategic bomber was gradually being taken over by the ICBM, and *Bear As* were therefore later modified to *Bear E/F* standard. It may be added that the Tu-95 also provided the basis for the Tu-114 *Cleat* transport aircraft, from which the Tu-126 *Moss* AWACS was derived.

At Tushino in 1961 *Bear B* appeared, with the glazed nose replaced by a large radome, and an AS-3 *Kangaroo* air-to-ground missile semi-recessed under the centre fuselage. This sub-series was the first to sport a flight-refuelling

nose probe. Tanking was originally provided by the M-4, but this is now being replaced by the Il-78 *Midas*. An ELINT blister is sometimes seen on the right side of the rear fuselage of *Bear B*, but when blisters are present on both sides it becomes a *Bear C*.

Bear D was first seen in 1967, and is a Naval Aviation maritime patrol aircraft, produced by modifying a *Bear A*. It has an enlarged chin radome and an extremely large ventral radome, believed to be associated with locating naval targets and providing mid-course guidance for ship-to-ship missiles. In some cases the tail turret is deleted. *Bear E* is a maritime photo-reconnaissance derivative of the *Bear A*, with camera windows in the rear weapons bay doors.

Bear F is the first of the Tu-142 production series, characterized by an extended front fuse-lage with raised flight decking, a smaller version of the *Big Bulge* radar of *Bear D*, bulged nose-wheel doors, and (initially) with enlarged in-board nacelles. It is a glazed nose maritime reconnaissance and ASW aircraft, and it entered service in 1970. The *Mod 3* version (five pre-used

examples of which were sold to the Indian Navy in 1988) is distinguished by a MAD boom extending aft from the fin-tip. The *Mod 4* is similar, but reinstates the chin radar and has a thimble radome on the nose. It is reported to have a self-protection ECM system.

Bear G is a combined ELINT and strike version, probably produced by modifying the Tu-95 *Bear B/C*. It has two large pylons under the wing roots to take supersonic AS-4 *Kitchen* anti-ship/ground missiles, and the tail turret is deleted. It has a thimble radome between the nose radome and the refuelling probe. Around 50 are operational, according to *SMP-88*.

Bear H is the second Tu-142 model, though it lacks the fuselage extension. It has a medium-size nose radar, and front fuselage strakes to denote its use as a cruise missile platform. It can carry six 1620 nm (3000 km) AS-15 *Kent* missiles on an internal rotary launcher, and four more on pylons. The ventral turret is deleted. *Bear H* became operational in 1984, and the main operating base is at Dolon in the southern USSR, where a 14,000 ft (4300 m) runway is available. Over 70 *Bear H*s have been built, according to *SMP-88*. It is anticipated that during the early 1990s these aircraft will be armed with the much larger AS-19.

At time of writing the latest Tu-142 variant is the glazed-nose *Bear J*, which appeared in 1986, and is evidently responsible for ensuring continued VLF communications with missile-armed submarines in a nuclear war. It is thus Soviet Naval Aviation's equivalent of the US Navy's EC-130Q Tacamo and the later E-6A Hermes.

The Tu-142 is believed to have four 14,800 shp NK-12MV engines, and a gross weight in excess of 400,000 lb (180,000 kg). As a result of this

---

Regular observers during past NATO exercises, *Bears* are being seen less frequently in today's warmer political climate. *Bear Delta*, seen here, was the first version of the Tu-95 to have no provision for bombs or missiles.

INSET Cruising speed for the *Bear* is estimated by the US DoD at 442 mph or Mach 0.67, although higher speeds have been recorded. Each of those thrashing propellers has a diameter of 18 ft 4 in.

increased TOW, maximum radius is thought to have increased to about 4500 nm (8300 km).

Throughout the 1980s *Bears* have been operating over most of the world's oceans: over the Atlantic from Murmansk, Cuba and Angola, over the Indian Ocean from bases in the Yemen and Ethiopia, over the Pacific from airfields in the Vladivostock area, and over the South China Sea from Cam Ranh Bay in Vietnam.

RIGHT **Four current members of the Tu-95 family (designated Tu-20 and Tu-142 in service), top to bottom:** *Bear D* **naval missile targetting version;** *Bear F* **Mod 1 ASW variant;** *Bear F* **Mod 4 ASW variant; and** *Bear G* **cruise missile carrier.** (*Pilot Press*)

BELOW *Bear C* **was an early cruise missile carrier dating from the early Sixties. Note the** *Crown Drum* **I-band missile guidance radar under the nose and Elint blisters on each side of the rear fuselage.**

BOTTOM RIGHT **The** *Bear F* **series incorporated a number of major design changes to the wings and fuselage prompting the Tu-142 designation. The MAD sensor on the fin shows this to be a** *Bear F* **Mod 3.**

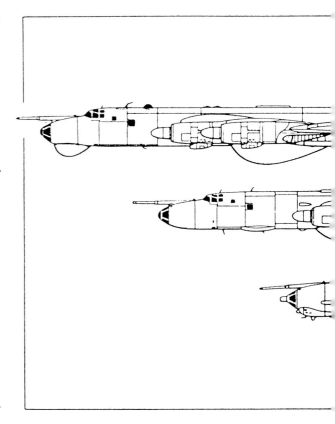

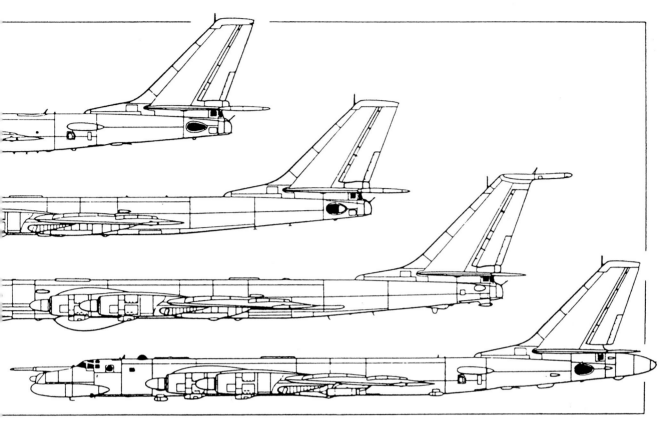

3 The First Supersonic Generation

As DESCRIBED in the previous chapter, in the first ten years following the end of WW2 Soviet day fighter design had progressed to the MiG-19, a lightweight twin-engined swept-wing transonic aircraft with a simple pitot intake on the nose. It was capable of exceeding the speed of sound in level flight only over a narrow altitude band, and reached a peak of Mach 1.36.

In taking the next step forward to aircraft with genuine supersonic capability over a wide altitude band, and peaking at around Mach 2, it was clear that an aerodynamically more slender airframe, a more sophisticated intake, and a higher thrust/weight ratio would all be required. If a worthwhile radius of action was to be achieved, then a relatively large fighter would be necessary, though this went against the traditional emphasis on large numbers of aircraft.

On the basis of supersonic wind tunnel research at TsAGI, the Soviet fighter design bureaus concentrated on configurations using two principal wing planforms: a highly swept and well tapered wing, and a simple delta. Whereas Western designers (notably Convair and Dassault) used comparatively lightly-loaded tailless deltas for supersonic fighters, the Soviets employed smaller delta wings that allowed a low-set tailplane to be retained.

Rather than relying on tunnel tests, full-scale comparisons of swept and delta wings were made by designing an aircraft that could accept either, although the internal centre fuselage structure presumably differed, according to the wing type. In one of the most remarkable development programmes of that period, the Mikoyan and Sukhoi OKBs together produced four major designs with swept and delta wings on aircraft of

two quite different size categories, the Sukhoi projects being heavier than the MiGs. Of these four, three went into production, and only the small swept-wing Mikoyan design (the Ye-2A *Faceplate*) was scrapped.

The Sukhoi OKB had been inoperative from 1949 to '53, but the staff were seconded to the Tupolev office, where they continued to work on fighters. The outcome was two series of designs: the S-series with swept-wings (62° leading edges) and the T-series initially with deltas. The first prototype of the S-1 flew on 8 September 1955 with a Lavochkin test pilot named Kochetkov at the controls. It made its public debut at Tushino on 24 June 1956.

The powerplant for the S-1 was the Lyulka AL-7, a comparatively large turbojet that first ran in 1952, and two years later entered small-scale production with a dry thrust of 14,330 lb (6500 kg). The non-afterburning AL-7 was used in several projects, including the Il-40 *Brawny* tactical bomber, but its principal application was the Beriev Be-10 *Mallow*. This was the world's first jet-powered flying boat to reach service status, and it may shortly be joined by the bureau's much larger A-40 Albatross, which was shown at Tushino in 1989.

Equipped with afterburner, the AL-7F produced a thrust of 19,850 lb (9000 kg). In the course of flight tests with the uprated AL-7F-1, Sukhoi's S-1 reached Mach 2.05 in late 1957, a speed that benefited from the use of a translating centrebody intake, the first in the Soviet Union. It also had a slab tailplane, and the pre-production batch introduced area ruling of the fuselage.

The high sweep made possible the use of a

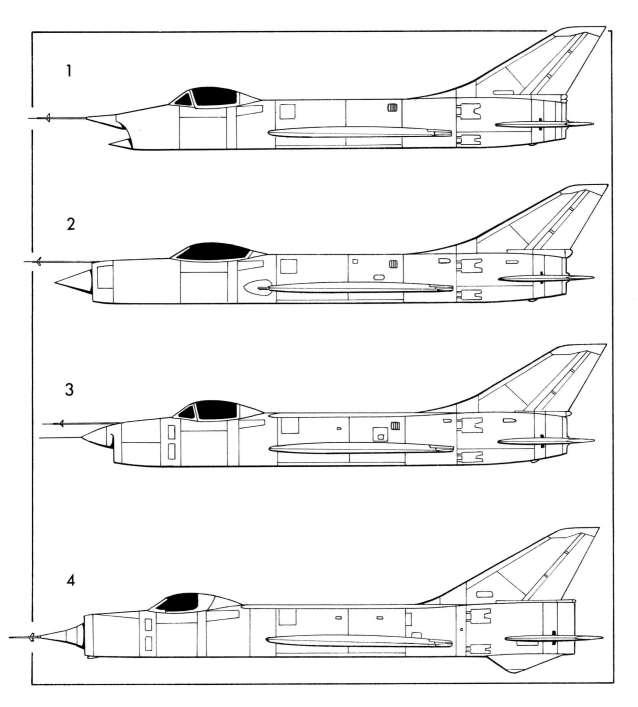

Sukhoi's T-series of delta-winged prototypes: 1, PT-7 with a rectangular inlet and variable lips; 2, PT-8 with large conical intake centrebody; 3, T-3 with chin inlet; 4, T-37 which flew in 1960.

relatively thick section and thus conventional construction, though the result (attached to ring-frames) was inevitably heavy. The main undercarriage units retract inboard, and appear to be shortened during retraction to clear the fuselage. This inboard retraction has the disadvantage of reducing the volume available for fuel, which is also restricted by the ducts from the nose intake.

The Sukhoi Su-7BMK, designated *Fitter A* by NATO, in standard Soviet Frontal Aviation markings. Under the port wing is an early ECM pod.

Sukhoi lengthened the fuselage forward of the wing to accommodate a second seat, thereby creating a dual control version of the Su-7; NATO called it *Moujik*.

Fitter A streaming its brake-chute from the prominent housing at the base of the fin. Range was always a problem with the Su-7 so in service twin ventral drop tanks were almost mandatory.
(*TASS*)

In consequence, the Su-7 *Fitter* is fundamentally short of internal fuel, and is generally seen with two pylon-mounted droptanks under the centre fuselage.

As for any aircraft with a highly swept wing, the Su-7 is short of external weapons hardpoints. It generally carries only two warload pylons, just outboard of the main legs. Other features include a 30 mm cannon installation in either wing root, an arrangement used earlier in the MiG-19, and one that minimises hot gas ingestion and pitching due to gunfire. The Su-7 also has four airbrakes distributed around the rear fuselage, a heavy arrangement, but one that is probably good from a trim-change viewpoint.

Series production is thought to have begun at Novosibirsk in 1957, a small number probably being built for the day fighter role before switching to the Su-7B *Fitter A* ground attack aircraft. Some 21 production aircraft appeared at Tushino in 1961. The series went through various modifications before production switched in 1970–71 to the variable-sweep Su-17 discussed in the next chapter.

The Su-7BM is believed to have introduced the 21,630 lb (9810 kg) AL-7F-1 engine, and the Su-7BMK was modified to give better compatibility with unpaved runways. It featured low pressure tyres, twin braking parachutes, and JATO provisions. All these aircraft are referred to as *Fitter A*. The tandem-seat Su-7U conversion trainer is known as *Moujik*.

The Su-7BM is estimated to have an empty weight of around 19,000 lb (8600 kg), which is approximately 25 per cent heavier than that for the 15,435 lb (7000 kg) Sepecat Jaguar, though considerably lighter than the 26,855 lb (12,180 kg) F-105D. Take-off weight is thought to be in the range 26,500–30,000 lb (12,000–13,600 kg). Maximum speed is widely quoted as Mach 1.6, thus this could be an underestimate, since the complexity of a variable-geometry intake would hardly be justified by such a speed.

To summarize, the Su-7 has a useful size for a ground attack aircraft, but its warload-radius performance is not as good as its weight may imply, due to its shortage of internal fuel and underwing hardpoints. In conversation with this writer in 1968, Soviet design engineers admitted that they had made a mistake in using these highly swept wings, and said that in future they would employ moderate sweep. Despite its shortcomings, the Su-7 seems to have been popular with its operators, as a very rugged aircraft that provides a stable weapons platform at high speed and low level. It has been used operationally by several countries, including Afghanistan, Egypt and India.

Fishbed

While the Sukhoi team began its project designs based on the massive AL-7 engine in 1953, the MiG design bureau commenced parallel studies based on the much smaller Tumansky R-11, which received the service designation R-37.

The R-11 was an unusual design, and it provided a useful insight into Soviet design philosophy for that period. It had a two-shaft arrangement, but only three compressor stages on either spool, each driven by a single turbine stage. This resulted in a very low pressure ratio (only 8.1:1 for China's WP-7BM version) and consequently a high SFC. Why two spools were considered necessary is not clear, though it may have reflected the major surge problems encountered with the RD-9B of the MiG-19. Although broadly comparable in thrust to the Rolls-Royce Avon, which has 15–17 stages on a single spool, the Tumansky R-11 is closer conceptually to engines intended for expendable drone powerplants, such as the 7-stage R-R Viper and the 8-stage GE J85.

The implication is presumably that the R-11 was designed for low cost and light weight, since

The Mikoyan team designed swept and delta-winged aircraft in their early work on a lightweight fighter that became the MiG-21. The swept-wing aircraft was the Ye-2A (above) code-named *Faceplate*.

The delta-winged Ye-5 became the predecessor of the famous MiG-21 *Fishbed*. Note the twin ventral fins that later gave way to one on the centreline.

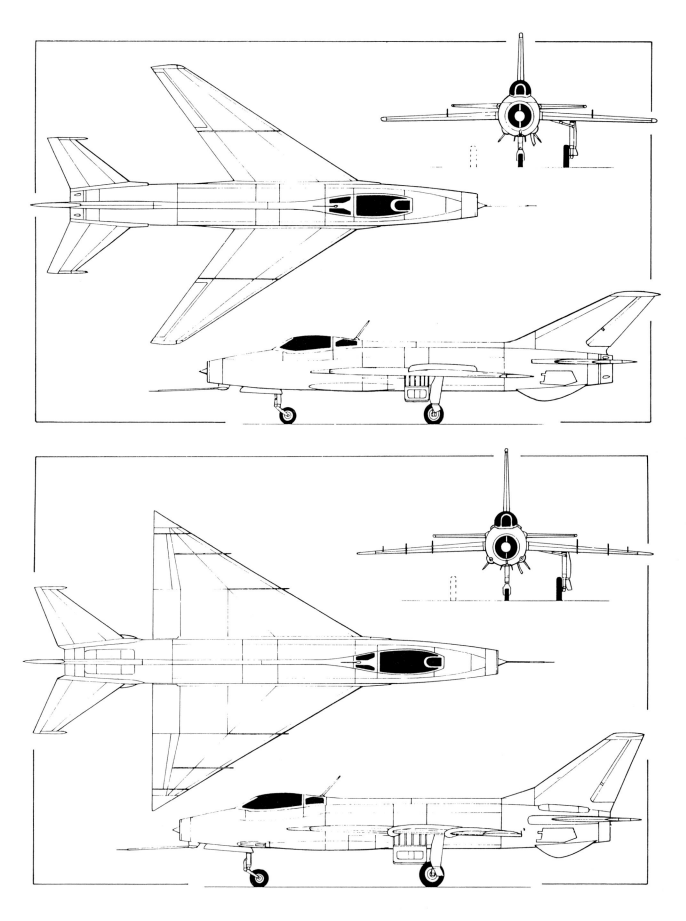

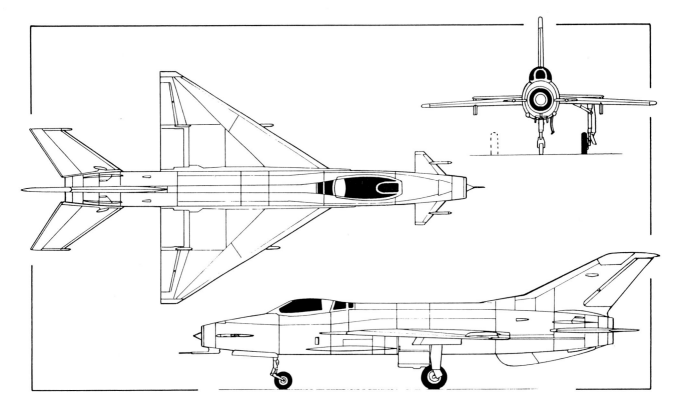

This unusual MiG-21 was an experimental airframe designed for a proposed close-support version. Designated Ye-8, it had moving foreplanes with anti-flutter weights to reduce rotation speed at increased weights.

it was to power a mass-produced short-range fighter, in which fuel consumption and endurance were of little importance. The R-11 was also probably designed with emphasis on wartime operation. The TBO has increased in stages from only 200 to 300 hr, and the 'total service life' of the WP-7BM is still only 600 hr. Accounts indicate that the R-11 is started electrically from an external source, using AVGAS from a separate tank for improved lightup in cold conditions.

The OR on which the Mikoyan design was based was issued in the autumn of 1953, and called for a clear weather high altitude interceptor, with emphasis on climb performance and high supersonic capability. It was to be equipped with radar ranging and armed with two lightweight IR-homing missiles, augmented by can-

non. In the early 1950s there was clearly an exaggerated belief in the effectiveness of small AAMs, since the F-104 was designed around a similar armament. The Starfighter was probably the closest Western equivalent of the MiG, but it was intended purely for air superiority, and it got off the ground slightly earlier, on 7 February 1954.

As in the Sukhoi case, the Mikoyan team designed swept and delta-wing projects using largely common fuselages and tail surfaces. They began with the tailplanes mounted rather high on the fuselage, Sabre-style, but the tail was soon brought down to a position only slightly above the plane of the mid-set wing.

First into the air was the swept-wing Ye-50, which flew in November 1955, and was followed one month later by the delta-wing Ye-4. The R-11 was not yet available, and it appears that the diminutive RD-9Ye of 8380 lb (3800 kg) afterburning thrust was used as a stopgap, augmented in the case of the Ye-50 by a rocket in the base of the vertical tail. Whether it was proposed to develop a mixed powerplant fighter on this basis is not clear. The Ye-50 is nonetheless reported to

LEFT A Tupolev Tu-95 *Bear D* cruises effortlessly at 29,000 ft (8840 m) over the North Sea on a maritime reconnaissance mission. In the absence of jamming, airborne and surface radars have little difficulty in detecting this impressive aircraft due to its sheer size and its 32 radar-reflecting propeller blades. *(Ian Black)*

BELOW *Jagdbomber-fliegergeschwader 37* of the East German *Luftstreitkräfte* operated this MiG-17F fighter-bomber (foreground) and MiG-15UTI advanced trainer from Drewitz airbase until October 1984. *(Harry Berger/MAPN)*

TOP RIGHT A back-seater's view of another Su-22U *Fitter G* operational trainer moving into formation with airbrakes deployed. *(Duncan Cubitt/AFM)*

TOP LEFT The MiG-21 *Fishbed* has worn the colours of more air forces than any other combat aircraft in history. This Hungarian AF MiG-21PF drew the crowds at Farnborough in 1990 *(Tony Holmes)*.

BOTTOM LEFT The definitive MiG-21 *bis* (an East German example of which is shown here) has the R-25 turbojet, a refined airframe and upgraded avionics. *(H J van Broekhuizen)*.

BELOW Su-22M-4 *Fitter K* of East Germany's *Marine-fliegergeschwader 28* flies a practice maritime strike mission. *(Duncan Cubitt/AFM)*

Wings at maximum sweep (62°), a pair of Su-22s display their wings and fuselage hardpoints; built-in armament is a single NR-30 30 mm cannon mounted in each wing root.
(Duncan Cubitt/AFM)

Visible in this view of an Su-22M-4 parked in a blast pen is the Laser Target Designator System (LTDS) window at the bottom of the nose inlet cone; the extended air data probe in front of the bullet-proof windscreen, underwing fuel tanks and the muzzle of the NR-30 cannon protruding from the port-wing root.
(Kai Anders)

RIGHT The MiG-23ML is equipped with a J-band *High Lark* intercept radar and a ventral IRST system—a combination of sensors which gives the fighter a limited look-down, shoot-down capability. *(H J van Broekhuizen)*

BOTTOM LEFT The Soviet Union's largest combat aircraft manufacturing programme of the 1970s and early 1980s was the variable-geometry MiG-23/27 series. Although many Soviet fighter regiments have re-equipped with MiG-29s, the *Flogger* family continues to serve in large numbers in both its air defence and ground attack guises. Distinguished from the MiG-23MF *Flogger B* by its much smaller dorsal fin, this East German AF MiG-23ML *Flogger G* taxies with its wings at mid-sweep (45°). *(Kai Anders)*

RIGHT **The MiG-23BN**
Flogger H **is a ground**
attack aircraft derived
from the MiG-23MS,
but using the front
fuselage and cockpit of
the MiG-27. The variable-
geometry intakes of the
MiG-23 series are
retained, but the
GSh-6-30 Gatling Gun is
replaced by the GSh-23L
two-barrel cannon.
(H J van Broekhuizen)

BELOW **The two-seat**
MiG-23UM trainer is
based on the MiG-23M/
MS airframe. The
canopies are hinged at
the rear (they are shown
here cracked open for
ventilation), and the
instructor has a mirror
system that is deployed
whenever the
undercarriage is down.
(Kai Anders)

have reached Mach 2.31, a remarkable speed at a time when Britain had barely got the subsonic Hunter into service.

In the spring of 1956 the R-11 engine became available, though afterburning thrust was then only a modest 11,250 lb (5100 kg). Equipped with this engine, the swept-wing Ye-2A flew in May, and the delta-wing Ye-5 flew on June 16th, with a pilot named Sedov at the controls. These aircraft had twin ventral fins and above-centre tailplanes, and were code-named *Faceplate* and

Fishbed respectively. They made their debuts at Tushino on 24 June 1956.

It is believed that by the end of that year the Ye-5 had been chosen for full-scale development, leading to the MiG-21, one of the most successful fighters of all time. Its story has already been told in various publications, hence it is only summarized here. It might be characterized as a Mach 2 F-5, ie an affordable aircraft that provided many air forces with air combat training until they could afford something more serious. Over 10,000 MiG-21s were built for service with more than 40 air forces, though less than 500 now serve with the SAF.

With relatively minor modifications the Ye-5 became the Ye-6T, the basis for the first major production series, the MiG-21F *Fishbed C*. This entered service with Tactical Aviation in 1960, about two years after the introduction of the

Fishbed C was the first major service version of the MiG-21. Early aircraft had the forward-opening one-piece canopy which later changed to a side-hingeing design.

F-104A into the USAF. Good photographs became available in the West when the MiG-21F-12 was exported to neutral Finland in April 1963, but the type was not available for Western inspection until an Iraqi pilot defected with his MiG-21F-13 (serial 534) to Israel on 16 August 1966. This aircraft was subsequently flown in Israeli markings, renumbered as '007'.

The MiG-21F was built in Czechoslovakia as the CS-106 and in India as the Type 74. It also served as the basis for China's Chengdu J-7, a licence agreement on the MiG-21F-13 having been signed in 1961. However, the technical data package was incomplete, hence the start of manufacture was delayed until early 1964. The first Chinese-built J-7 flew on 17 January 1966, but only a small number of this first model appear

The tandem two-seat MiG-21U trainer was given the name *Mongol* under the NATO Miscellaneous category. These two examples share the ramp with four MiG-21PFMs (*Fishbed F*). (*TASS*)

The late-series MiG-21PF was the first of the family to incorporate a broad-chord fin and rudder and was the last to feature the forward-opening canopy. Armament included a GSh-23 gun pack under the fuselage.

to have been delivered. An improved version, the J-7 II, flew on 30 December 1978, with an aft-hinged canopy, continuously-variable (rather than three-position) intake centrebody, a second 30 mm cannon, and a more powerful engine.

Returning to the basic MiG-21F, the intake centrebody is in this case automatically set in the aft position for speeds up to Mach 1.5, the centre position for the Mach 1.5–1.9 range, and the forward position for higher speeds. The wing has a 57° leading edge sweep, an area of 247.5 sq ft (23 m²), and a thickness/chord ratio varying from 4.2 per cent at the root to 5.0 at the tip. The main spar is at 33 per cent chord, and there are two unswept spars further aft to take loads from the undercarriage attachments and the trailing edge surfaces.

The forward avionics bay being given some attention by an East German mechanic. The aircraft is a MiG-21PFM with a MiG-21MF in the background.

Due to the small depth of the wing, the mainwheels are retracted into the fuselage, turning through 90° relative to the legs in order to position vertically beside the intake ducts. The flaps might be regarded as modified Fowler-type, increasing in area when lowered. The tail surfaces are 6.0 per cent thick, and a fin-mounted jack operates the tailplane, which has anti-flutter weights extending forward from the tips. The aircraft has three ventral airbrakes.

One highly innovative and not completely successful feature is the escape system of the -21F, in which the hood and windscreen (which are fastened together and trunnion-mounted at the front edge) act as a blast shield for the pilot.

When the hood is closed it is attached to the ejection seat via further trunnions. On ejection the forward trunnions are released, and the seat takes the transparency with it, to protect the pilot. This system is reportedly usable down to 360 ft (110 m), but it was later superseded in some MiG-21 variants by a conventional escape system, as low level operations became the norm. The change to a conventional hood and quarter-lights spoiled the pilot's foward view to some extent. The windscreen is de-iced with alcohol spray.

The MiG-21F is powered by an R-11F-300 with an afterburning thrust of 12,680 lb (5750 kg). Its empty weight is 10,980 lb (4980 kg), which is 15 per cent heavier than the 9588 lb (4348 kg) of the F-5E, and 6 per cent lighter than the 11,660 lb (5290 kg) of the F-104A. The thrust available to the MiG is approximately half-way between the values for the F-5E and F-104A, ie, 10,000 and 14,800 lb (4535 and 6710 kg). Take-off weight for the MiG-21F with full internal fuel and two AAMs is 16,200 lb (7370 kg), compared to

Atoll (AA-2) and *Advanced Atoll* (AA-2.2) formed the air-to-air missile armament of the MiG-21 series until the arrival of the more efficient *Aphid* (AA-8) in the late-Seventies. *Advanced Atoll* is the missile on the outboard pylons of this aircraft.

15,745 lb (7140 kg) for the F-5E and 17,320 lb (7855 kg) for the F-104A.

Maximum take-off weight for the MiG-21F is 18,080 lb (8200 kg), which probably corresponds to 4575 lb (2080 kg) of internal fuel, a centreline 110 Imp gal (500 litre) tank and two rocket pods. According to the brochure, the MiG-21F-13 is capable of Mach 2.0 over the height band 41,000–60,600 ft (12,500–18,500 m). Maximum climb rate is 25,600–27,600 ft/min (130–140 m/sec). Absolute ceiling is 63,300 ft (19,000 m) at Mach 1.85.

Maximum permissible speed is Mach 2.35 with two K-13 *Atoll* missiles, and Mach 1.8 with rocket pods. The aircraft is cleared to 7G, and has a maximum IAS of 675 knots (1250 km/hr). Carrying the centreline tank, the clearance is reduced to 6G and 540 knots (1000 km/hr) IAS. With 7 per cent reserves, ferry range is 760 nm (1400 km), or 905 nm (1670 km) with the centreline drop tank, assuming it is jettisoned when empty. The corresponding figures for endurance are 1 hr 43 min, and 2 hr 03 min. Normal take-off run with afterburner is 2600 ft (800 m), and landing run with drag chute is 3000–3200 ft (900–980 m).

The two-seat MiG-21U *Mongol A* made its first flight in 1960, and entered production four years later. It retained the R-11F-300 engine, but the gun was deleted. The modern descendant of the MiG-21U is China's Guizhou FT-7, which first flew on 5 July 1985 and made its airshow debut at Le Bourget in June 1987. It differs from the Soviet original in having the Wopen WP-7BM engine, two ventral fins and provisions for a 23 mm twin-barrel Type 23-3 cannon under the fuselage. Empty weight is 11,750 lb (5330 kg). With 4170 lb (1891 kg) of internal fuel and two PL-2

AAMs, it weighs 16,736 lb (7590 kg). Adding a 176 Imp gal (800 litre) centreline tank gives the maximum take-off weight of 18,965 lb (8600 kg). Maximum speed is Mach 2.05, and service ceiling is 56,750 ft (17,300 m). Ferry range with the big tank is 700 nm (1300 km). The aircraft is cleared to 7G. Major overhauls are required at 600 hr intervals, and 'total service life' is 1800 hr.

In Soviet service the single-seater has gone through a multi-stage improvement programme, of which it is possible to mention here only a few of the highlights. The MiG-21PF *Fishbed D* was based on the Ye-7 prototype, and introduced a search radar, referred to variously as the Sapphire, RR-9 and R1L. It also features the 13,120 lb (5950 kg) R-11F2-300 engine, and an enlarged dorsal spine that houses fuel. Its pitot-static boom is mounted above an enlarged intake.

With the 13,670 lb (6200 kg) R-11F2S-300 engine and blown flaps to reduce attitude (and thus improve the view) in the approach, it became the MiG-21PFS, and with a conventional fixed windscreen and quarterlights, the MiG-21PFM. This led to the MiG-21PFMA or simply -21MA (*Fishbed J*), which has *Jay Bird* radar, two extra wing pylons, a larger spine, and provisions for the twin-barrel GSh-23 cannon. The new outboard pylons carry either droptanks or the AA-2C radar-homing version of *Atoll*.

The MiG-21MF that first flew in 1967 and entered service in 1969 retains the *Fishbed J* designation, but introduces the 14,550 lb (6600 kg) R-13-300 engine, which has a 300 hr TBO. Some of these aircraft visited Rheims in France in 1971, following which some data was published, possible accurate. Empty weight was given as 12,880 lb (5843 kg), and with the GSh-23 and four K-13s the type was reported to take off at 18,078 lb (8200 kg). With two K-13s and three

Kitted out in a pressure suit that would be considered outdated by Western standards, a Soviet Frontal Aviation MiG-21 pilot gives a 'thumbs up' for the camera. Like most Soviet fighters of the period, forward view is poor, being impeded by the high glareshield, gunsight, mirrors, etc. (*TASS*)

110 Imp gal (500 litre) droptanks, it reached its maximum take-off weight of 20,723 lb (9400 kg). Maximum speed was given as Mach 1.06 at sea level and Mach 2.1 at altitude. Service ceiling was stated to be 59,000 ft (18,000 m). The MiG-21M is an export version of the -21MF, but powered by the R-11F2S-300 engine, and built in India as the Type 96.

On 9 December 1970 Artem I Mikoyan died at the age of 65, and was replaced as head of the bureau by Rostilav A Belyakov. Mikhail I Gurevich survived to 1976, but had retired in 1964 at the age of 71.

The first flight of the MiG-21bis *Fishbed L* took place in 1971. The structure had been extensively re-engineered to provide a longer fatigue life, and it was equipped with integral tanks, updated avionics, and the 16,535 lb (7500 kg) R-25-300 engine. An enlarged spine tank took total internal capacity to 638 Imp gal (2900 litres). *Fishbed N* is an advanced version of the MiG-21bis, with modified avionics and a different missile fit. It carries the semi-active radar-homing AA-2C *Atoll* outboard, and the AA-8

MiG-21MF or *Fishbed J* has a maximum speed of Mach 1.06 at sea level and Mach 2.1 at altitude. The prominent fairing mid-way along the fuselage above the wing houses the main undercarriage wheel.

Aphid inboard. Maximum take-off weight has been reported as 22,050 lb (10,000 kg), though it is not clear how this weight would be achieved. Some SAF MiG-21s have recently been equipped with retractable flight refuelling probes on the right front fuselage.

The MiG-21 series have been employed operationally in a number of small conflicts, including the Middle East wars of 1967 and '73, the Indo-Pakistan War of December 1971, and the long-running fight in Angola. However, none of these actions appear to have produced any definitive conclusions regarding its usefulness in air combat. Although never officially confirmed, it is widely believed that in the 1967 Six-Day War a flight of Algerian MiG-21Fs landed at El Arish airfield, which had just been captured by the Israelis. Two or three were reportedly dissembled and flown out in C-130s for USAF testing at WPAFB.

In Vietnam the MiG-21 appeared in late 1965. From ground photographs the Soviet-supplied MiG-21PF appears to have been the type mainly used. It was employed primarily in rear-aspect attacks with K-13 missiles against US strike formations, the MiGs generally flying straight through in pairs at around Mach 1.4. By May 1972 the NVNAF had reached a total of approximately 200 MiGs, of which 93 were MiG-21s, 33 were MiG-19s, and the remainder were MiG-17s and -15UTIs. At that stage the MiG-21 was armed

with the 23 mm gun in place of the original single-barrel 30 mm, and four K-13s. Of the total of 184 MiGs shot down by the US services, 82 were MiG-21s.

The US assessment of the MiG-21 was that it was superior to the F-4 in terms of low-speed manoeuvrability and acceleration at all altitudes, and at high supersonic speeds above 25,000 ft (7600 m). On the other hand the F-4 was generally superior below 20,000 ft (6100 m), and had a much better zoom capability. The F-4 is, of course, an infinitely more versatile aircraft, having been used operationally for air superiority, close support and interdiction.

From a pilot's viewpoint, the MiG-21 appears to have been generally popular for its vice-free handling, although there have been critical remarks about not having sufficient fuel to confirm the claimed maximum speed or service ceiling. It has also been criticized for its heavy stick forces (a traditional Soviet feature), poor instruments and GGS, limited radar range, and a cabin conditioning system that is quite inadequate for hot climates.

From a designer's viewpoint, the MiG-21

extracts a good performance from a relatively small engine, and its basic configuration is aerodynamically innovative. However, its small size severely restricts its usefulness, and the small number of pylons (five at most), coupled with the need for external fuel and its highly uneconomical engine give it appalling warload-radius performance. To be fair, it does what was intended in the original OR quite cheaply, and it may be quite useful in the tactical reconnaissance role. The SAF is thought to retain around 50 MiG-21R/RF *Fishbed Hs*, photo-reconnaissance versions of the MiG-21PFMA/MF.

In late 1988 the Soviets reportedly offered India yet another stage of MiG-21 development, using the 18,300 lb (8300 kg) Isotov RD-33 turbofan from the twin-engined MiG-29. This derivative would have a chin intake, allowing a larger nose radar, and an enlarged wing. The idea of a larger wing must be very attractive, as weights have increased considerably from the 18,080 lb (8200 kg) maximum of the MiG-21F to the reported 22,050 lb (10,000 kg) of the MiG-21bis, and the obviously even heavier RD-33-engined derivative.

Relatively early variants of the MiG-21 are still being built at Chengdu, where current models include the J-7 II and the limited all-weather J-7 III. The latter programme was launched in 1981, and the first prototype first flew on 26 April 1984, with somewhat more power and an en-

Three-view drawing of the MiG-21SMT (*Fishbed K*), which is considered by some to be the first of the 'third generation' series of the family.
(*Pilot Press*)

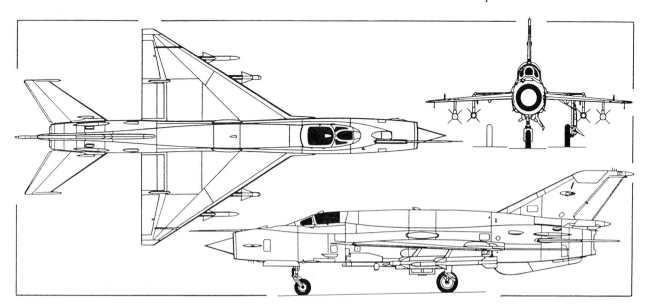

larged intake. Reports indicate that approximately 500 MiG-21s have been exported under the F-7 designation, recent customers including Pakistan and Bangladesh.

The current F-7M 'Airguard' is powered by a 13,450 lb (6100 kg) WP-7BM. It differs visibly from the Soviet original in having two 30 mm cannon (each firing at 840 rd/min), a conventional windscreen and quarterlights arrangement, a pitot-static boom above the intake, and two additional wing pylons (relative to the MiG-21F), which are normally used to carry droptanks. It also differs in having a conven-

ABOVE AND BOTTOM LEFT Similar in appearance to the MiG-21U is China's Guizhou FT-7 which first flew in July 1985. Unlike its Soviet counterpart, the FT-7 has twin ventral fins and dual missile and gun armament as well as internal changes.

tional ejection seat, a GEC Avionics HUD-WAC, and a new radar ranging equipment, ADC, radar altimeter and VHF/UHF radio.

The F-7M has an empty weight of 11,630 lb (5275 kg) and takes off at 16,505 lb (7531 kg) with two PL-7 AAMs. It has a maximum climb rate of 35,400 ft/min (180 m/sec), a service ceiling of 59,700 ft (18,200 m), and a maximum speed of Mach 2.05 with two PL-7s. It is cleared to 7G. Sustained turn rate is given as 14.7 deg/sec at sea level and Mach 0.7, and 9.5 deg/sec at 16,400 ft (5000 m) and Mach 0.80. With three tanks and two PL-7s it has a CAP endurance of 40 min with

TOP LEFT In 1962, China imported the MiG-21F and subsequently manufactured the type under the designation F-7. These appear to be early aircraft as the improved F-7 II has a rear-opening canopy and fixed windscreen.

5 min combat allowance, or can intercept at a radius of 350 nm (650 km), including a Mach 1.5 dash. With three tanks and two 330 lb (150 kg) bombs it has a HI-LO-HI radius of 325 nm (600 km). Ferry range is 1200 nm (2230 km).

There are several variations on the F-7M theme, including the F-7P 'Skybolt' for Pakistan, but the next major step on current planning will be the 'Super-7' with lateral intakes and a modified wing. A joint effort with Grumman and the Pakistan Aeronautical Complex, this programme was suspended in June 1989 as part of a US protest against repression in China. However, CATIC is still showing a model of the 'Super-7' at international airshows, and provides the following data, although the engine has not yet been chosen. Nominal gross weight is 19,400 lb (8800 kg), and maximum take-off weight is 23,800 lb (10,800 kg). Maximum speed is in excess of Mach 1.8, and ceiling is 59,000 ft (18,000 m). Design load factor is 8.5G.

Big MiGs

Although the Mikoyan team's principal successes in this period related to the lightweight MiG-21 series, the bureau simultaneously developed some heavier prototypes, based mainly on the 18,500 lb (8400 kg) Klimov VK-3 engine and the 20,500 lb (9300 kg) Lyulka AL-7F, and using both swept and delta wings.

The aim was presumably to compete with Sukhoi in the heavier fighter category, although in this respect the Mikoyan team was unsuccessful. With hindsight, it may appear that the second half of the 1950s was the period in which the Sukhoi bureau gained the ascendancy, although this fact was not to be appreciated in the West for a further three decades.

As far as the Soviet Union was concerned, the

One of the big fighter prototypes built and flown by Mikoyan in the fifties was the I-75F. This dispensed with guns in favour of AAMs which appear to be precursors of the later *Anab* (AA-3). The I-75F was not proceeded with.

principal outcome of this larger Mikoyan family was the delta-wing Ye-166A record-breaker, which is now in the Monino Museum. Powered by a 22,000 lb (10,000 kg) class Tumansky P-166 (which was to provide the basis for the Mach 2.8 MiG-25), on 7 July 1962 it covered a 15/25 km course at a world speed record of 2681 km/hr, corresponding to around Mach 2.53. Over the same course on September 11th that year, it recorded a sustained altitude of 74,360 ft (22,670 m).

In a more practical vein, the Ye-152A *Flipper* was a long-nosed delta-wing aircraft, reported to be powered by two 12,675 lb (5750 kg) R-11Fs. It first flew in 1959, appeared at Tushino in 1961, and then disappeared from view. It seemed at the time to have significant potential, combining the basic configuration of the MiG-21 with a much

RIGHT No centrally-heated hall of fame for this famous aircraft. The record-breaking Mikoyan Ye-166A has to endure the harsh Russian winter outside at the Monino Museum where it now resides; this view shows it in a kinder setting. (*TASS*)

more useful size. However, it is now believed that it was abandoned in favour of the Su-15 (discussed later in this chapter), primarily because the latter had side intakes, permitting a much larger nose radome.

Although the Ye-152A proved a dead-end for the Soviets, development was taken up by the Shenyang Aircraft Co in 1964, leading to first flight of the J-8 *Finback* on 5 July 1969. Over the next 10 years test flying continued at a low rate, accumulating only 663 hr in the course of 1025 flights. In 1979 small-scale production was authorized for the day fighter role, since no radar was available. Meanwhile an improved version, the J-8 I, equipped with a Sichuan SR-4 radar, was being developed, and three prototypes were duly constructed. Strangely, the first was written off on 25 June 1980 prior to first flight, and the

When seen at Le Bourget in 1989, the Chinese F-8 II was considered by some observers to be rather a pedestrian aircraft, lacking in refinement and badly needing a good intercept radar to exploit its performance capabilities.
(*Barry Wheeler*)

second aircraft began the flight test programme on 24 April 1981. Small-scale production was authorised in July 1985.

Meanwhile a more extensive redesign was taking place, to introduce lateral intakes (Phantom-style) and thus allow a larger nose radar, the general objective being to form a high-low mix with the J-7 low/medium altitude fighter. The resulting J-8 II (serial 840612) *Finback B*, powered by two WP-13A II turbojets derived from the WP-7 (R-11F-300) by the Guizhou team, had its maiden flight on 12 June 1984.

When the fourth of six prototypes made its airshow debut at Le Bourget in June 1989, it was stated by CATIC that production deliveries had begun in 1987. The line was said to be running at only one aircraft per month due to funding restrictions, and around 20 had been completed by mid-1989. At the end of that year both models were reportedly being built in 'economical' batches, rather than in continuous production.

As inspected at Paris in 1989, the J-8 II appeared to be an unusually unrefined aircraft, differing from the Ye-152A not only in intake design, but also in having a single ventral fin

(folding to the right for take-off and landing, in the style of the MiG-23/27), rather than two large fixed strakes. The aircraft was presented statically with six bombs on the centreline pylon, four PL-3 IR-homing missiles on underwing pylons, and two rocket pods on two further outboard pylons. A 23 mm twin-barrel cannon with 200 rounds was installed ahead of the centreline pylon. It was reported that the aircraft can alternatively take PL-4 semi-active radar AAMs and an unspecified anti-ship missile.

The CATIC leaflet for the export F-8 II gives a wing area of 454 sq ft (42.2 m²), ie, 83 per cent more than the MiG-21. Empty weight is 21,653 lb (9820 kg), normal take-off weight is 31,530 lb (14,300 kg), and maximum is 39,250 lb (17,800 kg). Maximum speed is Mach 2.2, and maximum IAS is 700 knots (1300 km/hr). Service ceiling is 65,600 ft (20,000 m), and maximum range is a modest 1200 nm (2200 km). Take-off run is 2200 ft (670 m), with unstick at 175 knots (325 km/hr). Landing run with braking parachute is 3300 ft (1000 m). The F-8 II is powered by two Liyang WP-13A II engines of 14,827 lb (6725 kg) afterburning thrust.

In August 1987 Grumman was awarded a contract by the USAF to integrate a new avionic system for the J-8 II, including a modified Westinghouse APG-66 radar from the F-16A/B, a Litton LN-39 inertial navigator, a HUD and digital databus and computers. This Peace Pearl FMS programme, potentially worth $500 million, resulted in two J-8 IIs being delivered to Long Island in March 1989 to be equipped with the Grumman-integrated system and subsequently tested at WPAFB. Some 55 modification kits were then to be delivered to China between 1990 and '95 for incorporation in PLAAF aircraft, the aim being to deter Soviet reconnaissance flights over China.

However, like other US technology transfer projects involving China, Peace Pearl was put on ice following the Tiananmen Square massacre in Beijing in June 1989. At time of writing the programme appears to have been abandoned. Aside from this proposed avionics upgrade, CATIC representatives have spoken of improvements including a switch to the GE F404 engine (as used in the F/A-18) and the introduction of leading edge flaps to improve subsonic manoeuvrability.

Night/All-Weather

At a time when Britain was coming round to the idea of terminating further work on manned interceptors (ref DWP-57), the Soviet Union was making major efforts to improve defence against the nuclear bomber. As mentioned at the beginning of this chapter, during the mid-1950s the Sukhoi OKB produced a number of delta-wing research aircraft, known as the T-series, the first of which (T-3) flew in early 1956. The outcome (in parallel with the Su-7 swept-wing ground attack aircraft) was the delta-wing Su-9 *Fishpot*. It was ordered into production as an interim supersonic night/all-weather interceptor for the Air Defence Force, and entered service in 1959. Attempts were made to intercept high-flying U-2s with the Su-9, but without success.

Like the Su-7B, the Su-9 was powered by the 19,850 lb (9000 kg) Lyulka AL-7F, and was equipped with the R1L radar used in the

MiG-21PF. The early production *Fishpot B* was normally seen with two ventral tanks and four wing-mounted K-5M AA-1 Alkali beam-riding missiles, as used on the earlier MiG-19PM. A two-seat trainer designated Su-9U was also built.

The Su-9 is believed to have been the basis for the T-405 record-breaker, in which a pilot named Adrianov established a 100 km closed circuit speed record of 2091 km/hr (approximately Mach 1.97) in May 1960.

The 1961 Tushino flypast witnessed the debut of a new version of this aircraft, the Su-11 (T-4) *Fishpot C*, which is believed to have entered service in 1966. It differs basically in having an enlarged and lengthened nose to house the Uragan 5B *Skip Spin* radar, and to accommodate the increased mass flow of the 21,630 lb (9810 kg) AL-7F-1 engine. The standard armament was switched to two AA-3 *Anab* semi-active radar homing missiles. It is thought that a combined total of about 2000 Su-9s and -11s were built, and that several hundred were later converted for use as target drones.

It seems likely that the T-431 record-breaker was a modified Su-11. On 4 July 1959 this aircraft established a zoom altitude record of 94,635 ft (28,852 m). A pilot named Kozlov later set a 500 km closed circuit record speed of 2337 km/hr (approximately Mach 2.20). In September 1962 the T-431 piloted by Vladimir Ilyushin established a sustained altitude record of 69,435 ft (21,170 m), but later that month this was beaten by Mikoyan's Ye-166.

Although the Su-9 of 1959 represented an all-weather interceptor with high supersonic capability, its operational effectiveness was clearly limited by the nose intake, which restricted radome diameter, and by the fact that it was a single-seater. A larger aircraft with different intakes offered the prospect of longer target acquisition ranges, through the use of a larger antenna and a dedicated radar operator. Such a project would clearly be heavier and would require more thrust, which suggested a change to two engines. At the same time a need was developing for a high performance light bomber, hence R&D costs could be shared between two separate applications.

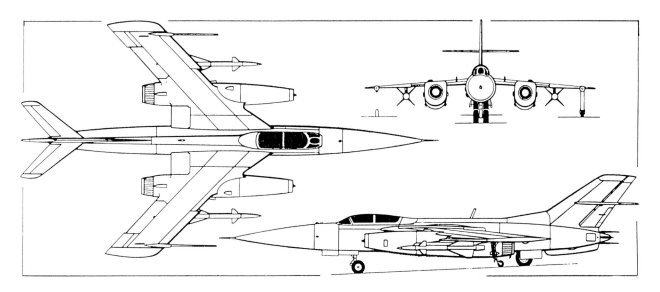

Yak-28P *Firebar C* which entered service around 1967. It had a longer nose and engine nacelles, while armament included *Anab* and later, *Atoll*. (*Pilot Press*)

The resulting Yak-28 *Firebar* was an interesting example of derivative design, broadly following the Yak-25 *Flashlight* configuration, though offering little or no commonality with its lacklustre forebear. Whereas the Yak-25 used non-afterburning RD-9s from the MiG-19, the Yak-28 employed afterburning R-11s from the MiG-21, giving approximately 130 per cent more static thrust. Rather than the zero-track tricycle undercarriage of the Yak-25 (in which the rear unit bore most of the aircraft weight), the Yak-28 introduced a true Boeing-style bicycle arrangement, the rear unit being placed much further aft to give the strike version (*Brewer*) an internal weapons bay. In the case of the interceptor, this bay is assumed to be used for additional fuel

To replace the Yak-25 *Flashlight*, the Yakovlev Bureau developed the much improved Yak-28 series for use both as an all-weather interceptor (above) and as a strike aircraft. NATO called the fighter version *Firebar*.

tanks. Due to the need for depth in this comparatively narrow bay, the wing of the Yak-28 is set much higher on the fuselage than in the case of the Yak-25. Its area was increased by 30 per cent to 405 sq ft (37.6 m²), the wing was more sharply swept, and leading edge extensions were added outboard. In some photographs these extensions appear to be used as flaps.

The first production air defence version was the Yak-28P *Firebar B*, deliveries of which began in 1962. From 1967 deliveries switched to *Firebar C*, with a much longer nose, enclosing the *Skip Spin* Uragan 5B radar of the Su-11, longer wingtip booms (thought to act as anti-flutter weights), and larger nacelles, believed to house the 13,670 lb (6200 kg) R-11F2S-300 engines of the MiG-21PFM. This version can carry two AA-2 *Atolls* in addition to the main armament of two AA-3 *Anabs*, medium-range weapons that are used in both IR-homing and semi-active radar forms. Maximum rate of climb is thought to be similar to that for the MiG-21F-13, ie, up to 27,600 ft/min (140 m/sec). In the Pentagon's *SMP-89* the Yak-28 is credited with a maximum speed of Mach 1.8 and a radius of 485 nm (900 km) with two AAMs.

The pilot conversion trainer is known as the Yak-28U *Maestro*. It has no radar, and probably no armament provisions. The fact that it has two separate cockpits in tandem and small nacelles suggests that the Yak-28U is a converted early production *Brewer*.

A Sukhoi Su-15 *Flagon F* banks past its Swedish
Coastguard observer, the Soviet pilot extending the
four airbrakes on the rear fuselage to reduce his speed.
Under the wings are *Anab* AAMs.
(*FLYG vapen NJTT*)

On a somewhat later timescale than the
Yak-28P, the Soviets developed what became the
heaviest interceptor in the world, presumably to
combine a long endurance with heavy long-range
missiles and a transonic dash performance. The
Tu-28P *Fiddler A* had its debut at Tushino in
1961, when two prototypes took part. This initial
version carried two AA-5 *Ash* missiles, and had a
large dark ventral fairing and two large strakes
under the rear fuselage. It may be that the fairing
was intended to house some form of AEW radar,
which subsequently proved too difficult to develop. The next appearance came with Domodedovo in 1967, when three *Fiddler Bs* flew over,
each armed with four AA-5s (two with IR heads
and two with semi-active radar homing), but
devoid of the ventral fairing and strakes.

This production configuration is assumed to
gross up to 100,000 lb (45,000 kg), and to be
powered by two afterburning engines in the
26,500 lb (12,000 kg) ballpark, possibly variants
of the AL-21F. In *SMP-89* the Tu-28 is credited
with a maximum speed of Mach 1.5 and a radius
of 800 nm (1500 km) with four AAMs. The
Tu-28P is believed to have entered service with
Air Defence Force around 1968. The production
total may have reached about 200, but most
Tu-28Ps have now been replaced by more capable interceptors.

When autonomous operation was required to
carry out an intercept in the presence of jamming, then a two-seater such as the Yak-28 or
Tu-28 had a clear advantage over any single-
seater. However, when close control from the
ground was feasible, a single-seater could still
perform effectively, and at the same time could
provide a higher aerodynamic performance for a
given thrust.

Demands in the late 1950s for a high performance single-seat air defence fighter had already
produced the Su-11, but for high supersonic
speeds to be maintained while carrying large

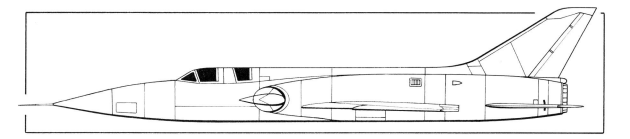

First flown in 1957 was the Sukhoi P-1 interceptor prototype. This was designed to carry a large radar with a battery of rockets in place of AAMs. Lateral intakes fed a single engine, although two engines were planned for production aircraft. The proposal was subsequently dropped.

missiles, a twin-engined aircraft was required. The Su-15 (T-5) *Flagon* that responded to this demand might be regarded as a twin-engined big brother to the Su-11, using a similar delta planform, but (originally) two R-11 engines as used in the MiG-21 and Yak-28. It was initially equipped with two AA-3 *Anab* missiles, and the Uragan 5B *Skip Spin* radar of the Su-11 and Yak-28. In this *Flagon A* form 10 examples were shown at Domodedovo in 1967, though they were probably preseries aircraft.

The first major production model is thought to have been *Flagon D*, which entered service in 1968, and introduced a double-delta planform and a conical nose radome. An unusual feature was that a short untapered section was inserted at the leading edge kink. This version was superseded in 1973 by *Flagon E* with improved avionics and the 14,550 lb (6600 kg) R-13F-300 from the MiG-21MF. The latest single-seater is the *Flagon F*, which entered service around 1975 and is distinguished by a shorter ogival radome. Two pylons near the wing roots are normally used to carry AA-8 *Aphid* short-range missiles to

Sukhoi Su-15 *Flagon F* three-view with additional side-views of *Flagon D* (top) and *Flagon G* (below). (*Pilot Press*)

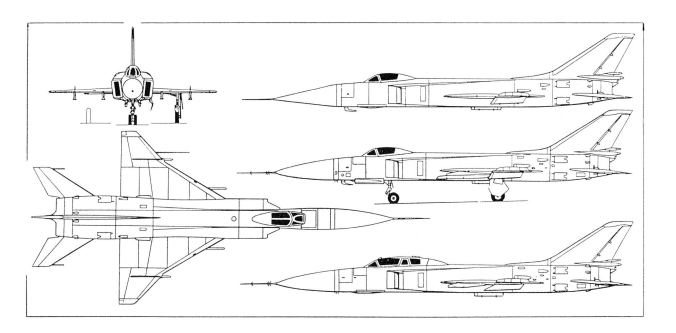

supplement the main armament of two AA-3 *Anabs*. Two underfuselage pylons frequently carry 23 mm gunpods; the Su-15 is one of the few Soviet fighters that does not appear to need external tanks.

The two-seat Su-15U began life as the *Flagon C* with a conical nose radome, but the current version is *Flagon G* with an ogival nose. The retention of the *Flagon* code-name indicates that these two-seaters retain an operational capability.

The Su-15 is comparatively large for a single-seater, grossing perhaps 45,000 lb (20,400 kg). In *SMP-89, Flagon E/F* is credited with a Mach 2.0 capability and a radius of 540 nm (1000 km) with four AAMs. It is estimated that over 1000 Su-25s have been built, and that around 400 remain in service, though these are being replaced by the MiG-23 and MiG-25.

The main claim to fame (or notoriety) of the Su-15 is that this was the type used to shoot down the Korean Air 747 (flight number KL007) en route from Anchorage to Seoul on 1 September 1983. Probably due to a fault in the alignment of its INS, or a crew error in inserting the coordinates of the destination, the 747 drifted north of its intended track and crossed the southern tip of Sakhalin Island. Soviet air defences evidently mistook the radar track of the 747 for that of a USAF *Compass Ball* RC-135 ELINT aircraft operating from Misawa in Japan. Two Su-15s were scrambled from Sakhalin, and the 747 was destroyed using an AA-3, with the loss of 269 lives.

The most spectacular development of the second Soviet postwar generation was the Mach 2.8 MiG-25 *Foxbat*, which (since the US did not proceed with the Lockheed YF-12A) became and remains the fastest combat aircraft in the world. Although the absolute speed record has been won by the SR-71A, the absolute altitude record for aeroplanes is still held by the Ye-266M, the prototype for the MiG-25M *Foxbat E*. On 31 August 1977 this aircraft was zoomed by Alexander Fedotov to the remarkable height of 123,525 ft (37,650 m).

Aerodynamically, there is no doubt that the SR-71A represents a more refined shape. However, the MiG-25 is just as noteworthy in its way,

since it combines Mach 2.8 performance with a relatively conventional configuration, providing a better turn rate and airfield performance. In essence, the SR-71A was a single-point design, whereas the MiG-25 was a more practical and operationally more flexible aircraft.

Full-scale development of the MiG-25 is thought to have begun around 1960, in response to a potential threat from the Mach 3, high altitude Rockwell XB-70. The Soviet programme may also have been due in part to admiration of America's high flying, deep penetration reconnaissance aircraft, the Lockheed U-2, one of which was shot down by an early SA-2 *Guideline* near Sverdlovsk on 1 May 1960. (Another SA-2 shot down a 'friendly' MiG-19). The Soviets were also developing their own high altitude reconnaissance system in the form of a high-Mach drone (the *Yastreb*), and they may well have considered that the US would probably produce a similar vehicle. The US equivalent of the *Yastreb* was, in fact, the Mach 3 Lockheed GTD-21B, which was launched from the CIA's M-12s and B-52s in the period 1964–68.

The powerplant for the MiG-25 was to be the Tumansky R-31, which is thought to have been used in 22,000 lb (10,000 kg) P-166 preseries form in both the Ye-166 record-breaker and the *Yastreb* reconnaissance drone. Being designed for high-Mach flight, the R-31 is mechanically a very simple engine, with a five-stage compressor driven by a single-stage uncooled turbine. It is mainly of steel construction. Like the P&W J58s in the SR-71A, the R-31s operate on special fuel, in this case designated T-6. At supersonic speeds water-methanol is sprayed into the intake ducts (a trick used in record-breaking F-4 flights) to allow more fuel to be burned and thus increase thrust without exceeding the maximum turbine entry temperature. The static afterburning thrust of the basic production R-31 is reported to be 27,000 lb (12,250 kg).

Lockheed adopted a very sophisticated and relatively high-risk approach to the design of the A-11, of which 70 per cent of the structure was titanium, a very advanced material in a 1960 timeframe. In contrast the Mikoyan team was evidently instructed to use a low-risk approach for the MiG-25, in order to achieve dependable

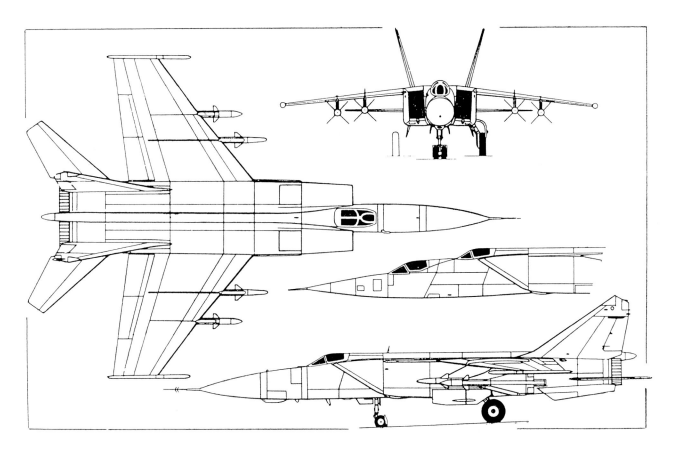

Three-view of the MiG-25M with four *Acrid* (AA-6) AAMs (two IR, two semi-active radar homing). The additional view shows the two-seat MiG-25U.

and quick results. The initial aim was to have an interceptor ready to match the entry into service of the B-70, which first flew on 21 September 1964.

The configuration adopted for the MiG-25 was therefore relatively conventional, being basically similar to the Rockwell A-5, though with a thin (4.4 per cent) low aspect ratio wing, and with two vertical tails instead of the Vigilante's lofty single fin. It may be true to say that the Mikoyan team pioneered the use of twin tails as a means to maintain directional stability at high AOA in the context of an aircraft fitted with wide Vigilante-style intakes.

However, instead of making titanium the principal airframe material, welded steel was used for the basic structure of the wing and tail surfaces of the MiG-25, with titanium restricted to the leading edges and aluminium alloys used for the trailing edges. Aluminium alloys are also employed extensively in the fuselage, with steel only in the hotter regions.

It is thought that the prototype Ye-266 first flew around 1964, and that the MiG-25 *Foxbat A* entered service with the Air Defence Force around 1970. At that stage it was equipped with the *Fire Fox* radar and armed with four AA-5 *Ash* missiles, though its armament was later changed to four AA-6 *Acrids*, using a mix of IR and semi-active radar homing heads. A Libyan *Foxbat E* has been photographed with a single AA-6 on either inboard pylon and two AA-8 *Aphids* on either outboard pylon, a somewhat surprising arrangement, as the Soviets are not as keen as the West on twin/multi-store carriage. As for other Russian single-seaters, the MiG-25 operates under tight control, using a data-link making inputs directly to the autopilot.

To put the development timescale of the

MiG-25 into perspective, the Lockheed A-11 had its maiden flight on 26 April 1962, and the SR-71A entered service in 1966, though there are reports that the CIA began operating the A-12 and the drone-launching M-12 in 1964. However, it should be borne in mind that the XB-70 had been reduced to research status in March 1961, hence the urgency had gone out of the MiG-25 programme at a very early stage.

Record flights began with the Ye-266 establishing a new speed record for the 100 km closed circuit in April 1965, but this was beaten by a YF-12 in the following month. Of the various published performances of the Ye-266, particularly noteworthy were the 500 km closed circuit speed of 2981.5 km/hr (approximately Mach 2.8) achieved by Mikhail Komarov on 5 October 1967, and the climb performance of 3 min 12.6 sec to 82,000 ft (25,000 m) attained by Pyotr Ostapenko on 4 June 1973.

The type make its public debut when four MiG-25s appeared at Domodedovo in July 1967, and two months later the West had its first opportunity to examine a *Foxbat A*, when on September 6th Lt Viktor Balenko defected with his aircraft from Sikharovka near Valdivostok to Kakodate airport on Japan's northernmost island of Hokkaido. The MiG-25 was subsequently returned to the Soviet Union, but it provided a great deal of information, as did Balenko himself.

The *Foxbat A* interceptor was followed around 1971 by the MiG-25R *Foxbat B* reconnaissance aircraft, in which the nose radar is deleted and replaced by five cameras and a SLAR installation. Whereas its predecessor has compound sweep (reduced outboard), this version has a straight leading edge. The conversion trainer is the

INSET Surrounded by a high fence, US and Japanese technicians begin to dismantle Lt Viktor Belenko's MiG-25 *Foxbat A* following his defection to Japan in September 1976.

LEFT Externally similar to *Foxbat A*, but operationally more capable, is the later *Foxbat E* or MiG-25M. The undernose laser ranger distinguished this variant from earlier types.

MiG-25U *Foxbat C*, with the radar deleted to allow the second cockpit to be inserted ahead of the existing pilot position. This two-seater appeared around 1974. The second reconnaissance version, the MiG-25R *Foxbat D*, has no cameras but an enlarged SLAR, and entered service around 1975.

The second phase of the interceptor programme came with the MiG-25M *Foxbat E*, which introduced uprated R-31F engines of 30,865 lb (14,000 kg) thrust and an improved weapons system, giving a limited look-down, shoot-down capability. In 1978 an official Soviet statement referred to a MiG-25 successfully intercepting a simulated low level cruise missile. The aircraft was flying at 19,700 ft (6000 m), the target was at a height of only 200 ft (60 m), and the firing took place at a range of 10.8 nm (20 km). This variant can be distinguished visually by means of a fairing (possibly for an IR sensor) under the nose. It is not clear whether *Foxbat E* is new-built or a modified *Foxbat A*, but it is known that the production line remained in use until the mid-1980s.

The latest known variant of MiG-25 is *Foxbat F*, which differs visually in having a dielectric panel just aft of the nose radome, and is believed to be a Wild Weasel defence-suppression aircraft, armed with the AS-11 *Kilter* anti-radar missile. It is thought to have entered service in 1988.

The enhanced climb performance of the MiG-25M was illustrated on 17 May 1975 by Fedotov's time (in the Ye-266M) of only 2 min 34.2 sec to a height of 82,000 ft (25,000 m), representing a reduction of 20 per cent on Ostapenko's climb time in the Ye-266 only two years earlier. As mentioned at the beginning of this chapter, Fedatov's zoom climb in the Ye-266M in August 1977 reached an altitude that has been surpassed only by balloons and by rocket aircraft launched from larger parent aircraft.

The MiG-25 is generally believed to have a maximum take-off weight of 80,000–85,000 lb (36,000–38,500 kg). Internal fuel is approximately 31,000 lb (14,000 kg). The *Foxbat A* is known to be redlined at Mach 2.8, but this probably reflects the conservative SAF attitude to any flight limit. *Foxbat B* has been tracked on radar at Mach 3.2. According to Pentagon sources, *Foxbat E* has a service ceiling of 80,000 ft (24,400 m) and a 740 nm (1450 km) radius with four AAMs.

At the time of Lt Balenko's defection, there were approximately 350 *Foxbat As* in service at nine bases, eight of which were in the Moscow area. It is thought that the Air Defence Force still has more than 300 *Foxbat A/Es*, and that there are perhaps a further 100 with Tactical Aviation, which also has around 150 *Foxbat B/D* reconnaissance aircraft.

Despite their high performance, the MiG-25 family are evidently regarded as purely defensive aircraft, and they have thus been exported relatively freely. Algeria is estimated to have 35 *Foxbat A/Bs*, India has 6 *Foxbat Bs* (as Canberra replacements) and two *Cs*, Libya has about 60 *Foxbat A/Es* and 6 *B/Ds*, and Syria around 80 *Foxbat As* and 8 *Bs*.

Light Strike

The derivation of the second generation Yak-28 *Firebar* from the early postwar Yak-25 *Flashlight* has already been outlined in the section dealing with night/all-weather interceptors. Prior to this, the Yakovlev bureau had also developed the *Flashlight B* light attack aircraft and the *Flashlight D* tactical reconnaissance aircraft. Each had afterburning engines and a glazed nose for the navigator/systems operator. They both appeared in prototype form at Tushino in 1956.

Of these Yak-25 variants, it is believed that only the reconnaissance aircraft was produced in significant numbers. However, with the development of the much heavier Yak-28, making possible much better warload-radius performance, the glazed-nose subseries also became worthwhile for the the strike/attack role. The result was given the ASCC designation *Brewer*.

At Tushino in 1961 one example of the Yak-28 *Brewer* was seen. It featured a small ventral bulge for the *Short Horn* mapping radar, a cannon on the left side of the front fuselage, and ventral strakes to smooth the air flow with the weapons

Brewer was the strike version of the Yak-28, this particular aircraft being *Brewer D*, a multi-sensor reconnaissance version. Pointed drop tanks were a standard feature of the type.

bay open. The main production version was *Brewer C*, which began replacing the Il-28s of Tactical Aviation around 1963.

The corresponding reconnaissance version was shown at Tushino in 1961 in the form of two development aircraft lacking the strakes of the attack model. In production this became *Brewer D*. The latest variant is *Brewer E*, an electronics warfare aircraft with what appears to be a cylindrical jammer pod half-submerged in the ventral bay. It also has less nasal glazing, no *Short Horn* radar, a variety of antennas, and two additional hardpoints outboard of the slipper tanks, presumably for anti-radar missiles.

The Yak-28 has not been exported, and in longer-range operations *Brewer* has largely been replaced by the Su-24 *Fencer*, but reports indicate that the SAF still has around 200 *Brewer D/Es* in service.

Bombers

Nearing the end of this chapter on the second generation of postwar Soviet military aircraft, we have seen that in the period 1955–65 the Soviets had flown supersonic combat aircraft in all the principal categories. They had also produced a variant of an all-weather fighter to perform the tactical nuclear strike mission. To complete the supersonic spectrum, all that was needed was a heavier bomber with a supersonic dash capability.

However, a supersonic bomber was an expensive undertaking at a time when the Soviet Union was spending large sums on ICBMs and SLBMs. The Soviets nonetheless made at least one attempt to develop a supersonic strategic bomber: the Myasishchev M-50 *Bounder*, a large delta-wing

OVERLEAF The Tupolev Tu-22 *Blinder* was first seen publicly at the 1961 Tushino display and created considerable interest due to its unusual rear-mounted engine location. Although supersonic, it was not the best performer in the bomber category.

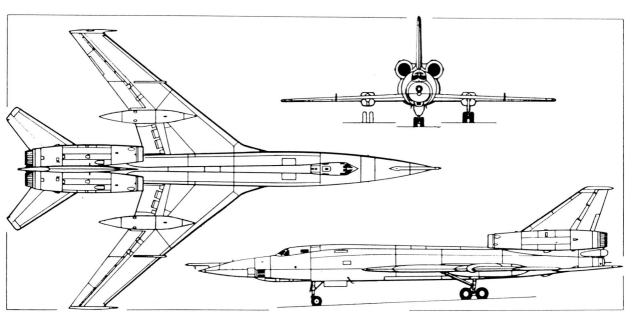

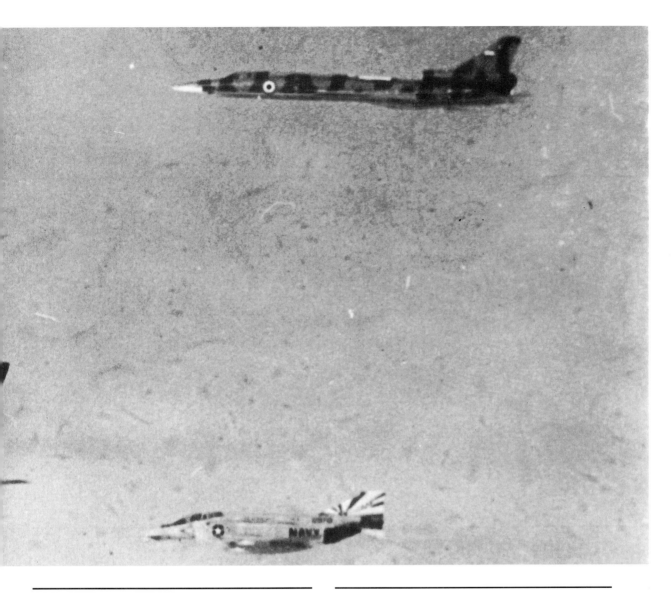

Libya was a recipient of *Blinders* in the mid-seventies and they have flown bombing operations against Egypt, the Sudan and Chad. These Tu-22s were intercepted over the Mediterranean in 1978 by a US Navy F-4 Phantom.

Tupolev Tu-22 *Blinder A*. Principal user of the type is now the Soviet Navy, the Tu-22M *Backfire* having replaced it in Strategic Aviation. (*Pilot Press*)

The Myasishchev M-50 *Bounder* was an attempt at producing a supersonic bomber. It did not proceed beyond the prototype state and the fourth aircraft (No 12) now sits at Monino alongside Sukhoi's bomber prototype, the Su-100.

aircraft with four Koliesov VD-7F engines, a bicycle undercarriage, and downward-firing ejection seats. The M-50 is thought to have flown in 1957–58, but (despite area ruling) probably offered only a marginal transonic dash performance at considerable penalty in radius, and thus never reached production status. It is relevant to note that in 1963 Nikita Kruschev assured British prime minister Harold Wilson that the Soviet Union had ended the production of strategic bombers, and this may well have been (temporarily) true.

In the intermediate-range category (ie, for European operations), the Soviets had continued their efforts, probably feeling that a supersonic dash capability was more important in that context. They made at least three attempts to develop such a bomber, but only one was successful. Two failures were the Tu-98 *Backfin* and the Il-54 *Blowlamp*, twin-engined aircraft that appear to have been based on optimistic wave drag estimates.

Soviet efforts were encouraged by the appearance of the delta-wing Convair B-58 Hustler, which first flew on 11 November 1956, prior to which it had been one of the best-kept postwar secrets. The B-58 was powered by four 16,000 lb (7250 kg) afterburning J79-GE-1 engines, grossed about 160,000 lb (72,560 kg), and had a Mach 2 dash capability. A total of 116 were built for SAC, but the type served only briefly.

It is believed that the full-scale development of the Soviet Union's first supersonic bomber to be produced in series, the Tu-22 *Blinder*, began around 1956. The first flight took place just before the end of the decade, and the Tu-22 began replacing some Tu-16s in the intermediate-range bomber role in 1961-61. A total of 10 Tu-22s were present at Tushino in 1961, of which one carried a large cruise missile. At the 1967 Domodedovo show, 22 Tu-22s appeared, mostly armed with the AS-4 *Kitchen* missile and equipped with a flight refuelling probe.

The Tu-22 has an unusual powerplant installation, its two engines being mounted in pods over the rear fuselage, on either side of the vertical tail. This location was probably determined by Area Rule considerations, which appear to have also played a major role in other aspects of the aircraft's design. The fuselage is waisted in line with the wing; the main under carriage retracts into trailing edge fairings.

The Tu-22 has a crew of three, who enter the aircraft via ejection seats that are winched up from ground level, implying that ejection is downward to avoid the problem of clearing the rear of the aircraft. Defensive armament is limited to a single gun, directed by *Fan Tail* radar.

The Tu-22 is believed to be equipped with two Koliesov VD-7Fs (in effect, half the M-50 power-plant), each producing an afterburning thrust of 30,900 lb (14,000 kg). The inlets seem to be sized for in-flight performance, with additional air supplied at low speeds via annular slots exposed by forward translation of the cowling lip. Gross weight is thought to be approximately 190,000 lb (86,000 kg). The aircraft is credited in *SMP-87* with a maximum speed of Mach 1.4 and a radius of 1565 nm (1900 km).

The initial production aircraft was *Blinder A*, armed with conventional bombs. This was superseded by *Blinder B*, with the AS-4 cruise missile and flight refuelling provisions. Some 170 of these aircraft are believed to have been delivered to Strategic Aviation. This version was followed by *Blinder C*, the Soviet Naval Aviation variant (around 50 delivered), with five camera windows and ELINT equipment. The pilot training version, the Tu-22U *Blinder D*, is flown in both the Soviet Union and Libya.

Although basically a sound design, the Tu-22 won only limited acceptance due to the development of the Tu-22M *Backfire*, which led to the Tu-22 being quickly relegated to reconnaissance and electronic warfare roles. Exports were restricted to Iraq and Libya, which are believed to have five and seven respectively at time of writing. Both are thought to have employed it operationally. Iraq has used it against Kurdish villages. Libya has used it against Tanzania, and in a remarkably effective raid against Chad in February 1986, in retaliation for the French Air Force bombing of the airfield at Wadi Doum. If the latter report is accurate, a single Tu-22 released a stick of four bombs from a height of approximately 16,500 ft (5000 m) over the main runway at the capital, N'Djamena, and all four hit, closing the airport for several days.

4 The Less-Long Airfield Generation

As DISCUSSED in the previous chapter, during the period 1955–65 the Soviet Union flew nine major new combat aircraft types, all capable of genuine supersonic performance at altitude. However, the Soviets could hardly rest on their laurels with this second postwar generation, since the West had already taken the initiative in regard to reducing airfield demands.

The aim of this line of development was initially to increase the number of airfields available to combat aircraft, and thus reduce their vulnerability to runway bombing, and perhaps ultimately to permit dispersal away from airfields that in war would become targets for nuclear weapons. To stay abreast, the next Soviet generation would have to combine the high-Mach capability of the second period with significantly shortened runway requirements.

Airfield performance could be improved either by increasing wing lift or through the use of jet lift to assist the wing. Considering the former option, the area of the wing could not be increased without penalising maximum speed, hence a higher lift coefficient would have to be achieved. At that time it was widely held that really high lift coefficients could not be obtained on a wing of moderate or high sweep, although with hindsight the need for low sweep may have been exaggerated. The use of short fields by swept wing aircraft was therefore considered to require variable geometry, which also offered potential gains in regard to higher penetration speed, reduced gust response, and extended loiter performance.

The two options thus boiled down to the swing-wing and jet lift. Britain had by 1957 invented the vectored-thrust engine (now known as the Rolls-Royce Pegasus), which allowed propulsive thrust to be turned to the vertical for take-off and landing. However, this approach involved an expensive development programme and an engine unsuitable for other applications. To minimize development costs and retain design flexibility, the Soviets rejected the Pegasus concept and opted instead for the use of dedicated lift engines, which in V/STOL projects would supplement the deflected thrust of conventional propulsion engines.

By varying the number of lift engines used, this concept (which basically follows German philosophy) could be applied to anything from a small close support aircraft to a large tactical transport. The big question they had to decide was whether to develop both swing-wing and jet-lift aircraft, or to concentrate on just one of these concepts. In the event, variable sweep was adopted for most combat aircraft of this third generation, but lift engines and deflected thrust were favoured for some naval developments.

At Domodedovo on 9 July 1967 the aircraft on show included two swing-wing types (the proto-types of the MiG-23 and Su-17) and three aircraft with lift engines (*Fishbed G*, *Faithless* and *Flagon B*). The fact that they had decided to make a full-scale comparison of the swing-wing and jet-lift means of reducing airfield demands was admirable, but it should perhaps be emphasized that they were not the main pioneers in either type of technology.

The big advance in the swing-wing field had been NASA's development of the outboard hinge concept in the late 1950s, using computer analysis to predict a locus of hinge positions to minimize aerodynamic centre shift. Prior to this,

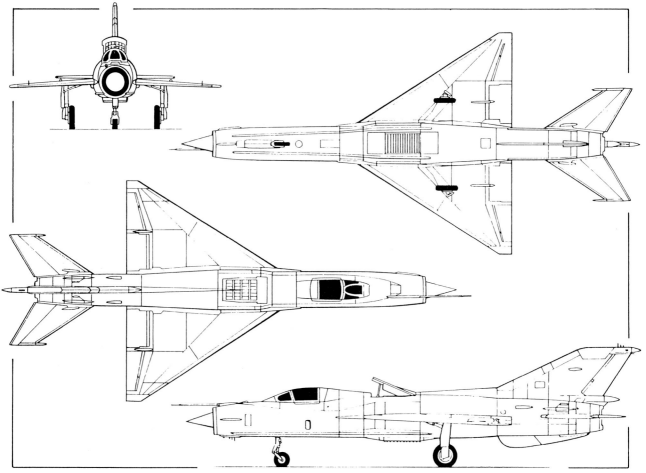

Mikoyan's Ye-23, dubbed *Faithless*, landing at Domodedovo in 1967 with its lift engines door open and wing trailing-edge flaps lowered.

it appeared that it would be necessary to use translating wing attachments, as was done on the Bell X-5 (first flight 20 June 1951) and the Grumman XF10F Jaguar (19 May 1952). The first production swing-wing aircraft was the F-111, which was rolled out in October 1964 and first flew on December 21st that year, followed by the F-14, which flew exactly six years later. In fairness to the Soviets, it should be added that the first European swing-wing aircraft was the Tornado, which did not fly until 14 August 1974.

Regarding the use of lift engines, the pioneers were Rolls-Royce. The Shorts SC.1, equipped with five RB.108s (four lifting, one propelling) made its first free hover on 25 October 1958 and completed its first transitions between jetborne

Fishbed G was a low-speed lift engine test-bed conversion of the MiG-21PFM and like *Faithless*, it made its only public appearance at the 1967 Domodedovo display.

and wingborne flight on 27 April 1960. Rolls-Royce lift engines were used in many V/STOL research aircraft, but Britain switched to the Pegasus vetored-thrust concept, the Hawker P.1127 making its first transitions on 12 September 1961.

Flogger

By the time of the Domodedovo show of 1967, it might thus be argued that jet lift was seven years old and practical swing-wing aircraft had been flying for almost three years. Nonetheless, the scale of Soviet effort directed at these new technologies was quite impressive, as was their decision to make full-scale in-flight comparisons.

The most fruitful of these comparisons related to Mikoyan's jet-lift *Faithless* (believed to have been designated Ye-23) and the bureau's swing-wing Ye-23IG. In essence, these represented two options for a MiG-21 replacement. The broad aims were to produce an all-weather interceptor and air combat fighter that not only reduced airfield demands, but also provided far better warload-radius than its predecessor, and a much better radar. Since the MiG-21 had entered service in 1960, the objective was presumably to have its successor in production around 1970, which implied a first flight three years earlier. The Ye-23 and -23IG are, in fact, both thought to have flown in late 1966 or early '67.

Although conceptually different in their means of stall-speed reduction, the two proto-types had a considerable degree of commonality in their fuselages and tail surfaces. The Mikoyan team had learned from bitter experience the limited usefulness of lightweight fighters, and also (from the Ye-152A *Flipper*) the restrictions on radar performance imposed by a nose intake. These new designs were therefore much larger than the MiG-21, and had lateral intakes, although the Ye-23 adopted Mirage-style conical inlets, while the -23IG followed the two-dimensional inlets of the Phantom. The conical inlets of the jet-lift design produced a well-rounded centre fuselage, on which a delta-wing was mid-set in the MiG-21 tradition. The two-

The Ye-23IG prototype for the successful MiG-23 series of variable-geometry combat aircraft; this aircraft is currently at Monino.

dimensional inlets of the -23IG led naturally into a rectangular-section fuselage, encouraging the use of a high-set wing, which in turn facilitated a straight-through wing centre section.

Why the jet-lift approach (Ye-23) was rejected has not so far been made public. Probably the use of lift engines was criticized for ground erosion and tyre heating, and for increased pilot workload and maintenance effort. It was also a more expensive approach, it was heavier, and it penalized fuel volume. In essence, jet lift is the only way to produce combat aircraft with ground rolls of less than about 1300 ft (400 m), but less demanding airfield requirements are better satisfied in this context by aerodynamic lift.

The Ye-23IG was thus adopted as the basis for the MiG-23 *Flogger*, although several more years were to pass before this aircraft would enter service on a significant scale. The Ye-23IG prototype, which now resides in the SAF Museum at Monino, was almost twice as heavy as the MiG-21, so it was designed around the 22,050 lb (10,000 kg) Lyulka AL-7F-1 turbojet, as used in late-model Su-7s. It is believed that the same engine type was retained for a pre-series batch of MiG-23s, delivered from 1970, and presumably employed to sort out any special operational problems associated with variable-sweep wings.

The NATO designation *Flogger A* applied to both the Ye-23IG and the preseries aircraft, the latter reportedly having the SAF names MiG-23S and -23SM. The former carried no external armament, while the latter had two pylons under the fuselage and two under the fixed wing 'gloves'. There is believed to have been a tandem-seat version of the MiG-23S, designated MiG-23UB.

Before considering the further development of

the series, it may be useful to summarize the principal design features of the basic MiG-23. Reports indicate that only three wing positions are employed, giving leading edge sweeps of 16°, 45° and 75°, according to Mach No. Due to the use of variable geometry, the main undercarriage is fuselage-mounted, retracting into the lower sides to leave space for a centreline store. Again unlike the MiG-21, the -23 has twin nosewheels with a large mudguard.

The shape of the tail surfaces also demonstrates a break from earlier Mikoyan practice, perhaps because Belyakov wanted to introduce some feature that historians would recognize as signalling the change of leadership within the OKB.

Aircraft operated by FA tactical regiments are camouflaged in a variety of schemes using greens, browns and greys. Unusually, the red star tail insignia on these MiG-23UM *Flogger C* trainers differs in size, perhaps indicating an attempt at 'toning down' visual cues.

The tips of the tail surfaces are sawn off at an angle to the line of flight, presumably to improve flutter speed, and the fin was given a large dorsal extension (though this was later reduced).

When the undercarriage is down, the underfin is folded to the right to improve ground clearance. A folding underfin was probably first used in the Lockheed A-11 of 1962, and (as mentioned earlier) has now reappeared on China's F-8.

The triple underfuselage airbrakes used on the MiG-21 were abandoned in favour of quadruple brakes distributed around the rear fuselage, Sukhoi-fashion. Rear view seems to have played no part in cockpit design, the philosophy evidently being that warning of rear attack would be provided by tail-warning radar, supplemented by a mirror carried on a structural centreline member extending the full length of the hood, which is obviously jettisoned prior to ejection.

The AL-7 engine series was relatively old by the time the MiG-23 appeared, and it was therefore replaced in the case of the first large-scale production model by the Tumansky R-27

turbojet of 24,500 lb (10,200 kg). This not only provided slightly more thrust, but it was also shorter and lighter. The resulting MiG-23M *Flogger B* differed visibly from the preseries aircraft by having massive leading edge extensions on the outer wing panels, a larger dorsal fin, a shorter rear fuselage, and a wing mounted further forward.

Due to the extensive nature of the redesign, service entry of the MiG-23M was delayed to 1972–73. The two-seat derivative is the MiG-23UM *Flogger C*. The R-27 engine is also thought to have been used in the MiG-23MS *Flogger E* export aircraft, which is characterized by a much smaller nose radome, housing the *Jay Bird* from the MiG-21PFMA.

A further engine change took place soon after the introduction of the R-27, which was replaced on the production line by the Tumansky R-29, initially with an afterburning thrust of 25,350 lb (11,500 kg). The R-29 reportedly has five LP and six HP stages of compression, a pressure ratio of 12.4, and a mass flow of 231.5 lb/sec (105 kg/sec). The R-29-engined MiG-23MF retains the *Flogger B* codename, but introduces the J-band *High Lark* radar and a ventral IRST sensor, together giving (for the first time on a Soviet fighter) a limited look-down, shoot-down capability.

One point to be emphasized is that the MiG-23 is primarily distinguished from its MiG-27 ground attack derivative (discussed next in this chapter) by its variable-geometry multi-shock intakes, and not by its nose shape. Thus the MiG-23BN *Flogger F* is a day fighter and ground attack aircraft, produced largely for the export market, with the front fuselage of the MiG-27. A limited number of MiG-23BNs have been operated by the Warsaw Pact air forces (and by India) with an improved avionics fit, indicated by the two RWR sensors on the lower front fuselage. These excrescences have given rise to the modified NATO designation *Flogger H*.

The oldest 'swinger' in service and still one of the finest low-level, all-weather strike aircraft in the world, the F-111 had a stormy ride due to technical problems early in its career.
(*Jon Davison*)

Less successful in gaining a production order than other variable geometry designs was the French Dassault Mirage G, seen here demonstrating its wing sweep capability. The *Armée de l'Air* opted instead for the fixed-wing Mirage F.1.
(*AMD-B*)

In August and September 1978 courtesy visits were paid to Finnish and French air bases (Kuopio-Rissala and Rheims respectively) by six SAF MiG-23s from Kubinka, near Moscow. These visits provided for Western observers the first sight of the MiG-23ML *Flogger G*, distinguished from the MiG-23MF *Flogger B* (which it superseded as the standard SAF aircraft) mainly by its much smaller dorsal fin.

The first opportunity for a Western service to test this variant came 11 years later, when on 11 October 1989 Major Adel Bassem of the Syrian Air Force defected to Israel, landing at Megiddo airstrip. In the subsequent evaluation pro-

ABOVE A shorter dorsal fin distinguishes the MiG-23ML *Flogger G* which superseded the MF in Soviet interceptor units. Under the moving outer wing panel is a fixed pylon for an additional fuel tank; this would have to be jettisoned for wing sweep.

BELOW Probably photographed over the Baltic, this fully-armed MiG-23MF *Flogger B* banks away with its wings at intermediate sweep. The large missiles are *Apex* (AA-7) and the smaller ones are *Aphid* (AA-8).

gramme it was found that its R-29B produced better acceleration than the F-16 chase aircraft. The aircraft was fitted with a data-link for GCI, and its *High Lark 2* radar was used to project an image on the HUD, rather than on a conventional radar scope.

In order to improve directional stability at high AOA, the MiG-23ML was later modified by the introduction of large notches in the wing gloves, producing the *Flogger K*. This model is also reported to have two variable-sweep pylons under the outer wings, and a somewhat smaller

Comparable to the Saab Viggen in weight and airfield performance, the MiG-23 is perhaps best regarded operationally as a rather small, short-field F-4. It is, however, noteworthy that the F-4 (which is superior in several respects) first flew on 27 May 1958, about seven years earlier.

BELOW Side-views showing (top to bottom) the standard MiG-23MF *Flogger B* interceptor, MiG-23UM *Flogger C* trainer, and MiG-23MS *Flogger E* export fighter.
(*Pilot Press*)

LEFT The final refinement in the MiG-23 interceptor series was what NATO called *Flogger K*. The centreline store is a 23 mm gunpod.

ventral fin. The first good photographs of *Flogger K* were obtained by the US Navy in 1986, when SAF aircraft of this type began operating from Can Ranh Bay in Vietnam. This is thought to have been the final version, production of the MiG-23 having ended in 1985.

BOTTOM LEFT Their canopies protected by covers to prevent damage during routine flightline work, these East German-operated MiG-23MFs were photographed towards the end of the Cold War years. In the background can be seen some of the base's hardened aircraft shelters.

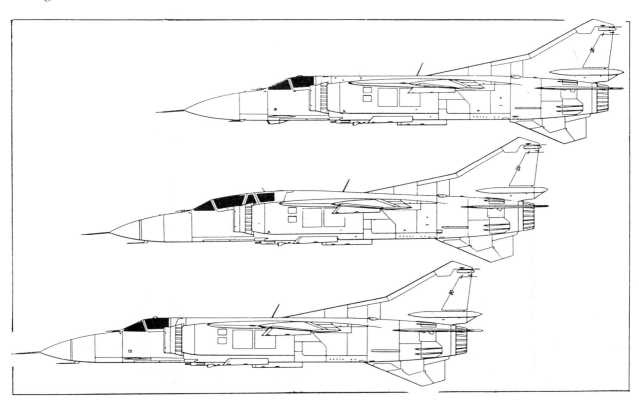

Though requiring considerable redesign in the course of development, the MiG-23 eventually proved highly successful and was built in very large numbers. Almost 2000 examples are believed to remain in use with the Air Defence Force and Tactical Aviation, and the MiG-23 have been flown by the air forces of Algeria, Angola, Bulgaria, Cuba, Czechoslovakia, Egypt, Ethiopia, East Germany, India, Iraq, North Korea, Libya, Poland, Syria and Vietnam.

Late production models have the R-29B engine of 27,560 lb (12,500 kg). There are provisions for water injection, though it is not clear whether this takes place in the intakes or the engine itself. Empty weight is approximately 23,000 lb (10,500 kg) in the case of the MiG-23ML, and the aircraft carries 10,140 lb (4600 kg) of internal fuel. It is often seen with a centreline 176 Imp gal (800 litre) tank, though reports suggest that up to five can be carried for the ferry mission. Iraq claimed in 1989 to have developed a flight refuelling capability for its MiG-23BNs, using a fixed probe ahead of the windscreen. Take-off weight for the basic intercept mission is approximately 35,500 lb (16,100 kg), but weight may reach 41,675 lb (18,900 kg) in the context of ground attack or ferry flights.

The MiG-23 has a fixed armament of one 23 mm twin-barrel GSh-23 cannon mounted under the fuselage. Additional armament may be carried on three underfuselage pylons, two pylons under the gloves, and (in some late-production aircraft) two pylons under the outer wings. Air-to-air missile fit originally consisted of four K-13 (AA-2 *Atoll*) weapons, but the MiG-23 is now seen typically with two R-23 (AA-7 *Apex*) medium-range weapons under the gloves, and two or four R-60 (AA-8 *Aphid*) short-range weapons on two pylons below the intake ducts.

Maximum speed at altitude is Mach 2.3, reducing to Mach 1.1 at sea level. Radius of action with six AAMs is estimated in SMP-87 as 620 nm (1150 km).

Ground Attack

The useful size and reduced-field performance of the MiG-23 naturally provided an excellent potential for the ground attack role. The MiG-27 (*Flogger*) appeared only shortly after the initial MiG-23 production series, being seen in East Germany as early as 1975. As indicated earlier, the MiG-27 is characterized by simple pitot intakes with small splitter plates, rather than the multi-shock intakes with massive ramps (with area suction) that are used on the MiG-23. The attack aircraft also has an R-29B-300 engine with a small afterburner and a two-position nozzle, whereas that of the MiG-23 is continuously variable.

The normal front fuselage of the MiG-27 differs from the original MiG-23 in that the radar is deleted, and the upper lines of the nose fall steeply to provide the best possible forward field

Four MiG-23BN attack/interdiction aircraft awaiting take-off. This version (*Flogger H*) is more usually associated with air arms outside the USSR, the type having been exported to Bulgaria, Czechoslovakia, India and Poland.

One of the more unusual weapon locations on a modern combat aircraft is the rear fuselage bomb crutch on the MiG-27 *Flogger J*, enabling it to carry four FAB500 bombs in either free-fall or retarded form.

of view, which is also assisted by a slightly raised eye position. Armour plate is added externally to the fuselage sides abreast of the cockpit, and there is probably further armour below the cockpit floor and ahead of the front bulkhead. The nose appears to house both radar ranging and a laser ranger, which may well have a marked-target seeker facility. Navigation is evidently based on Doppler radar.

The MiG-27 also introduced low-pressure tyres, requiring bulges in the undercarriage doors, and a six-barrel 30 mm Gatling-type gun in place of the GSh-23. Two bomb pylons were added under the rear fuselage, and these seem to be so far aft of the CG that they may well require an automatic pitch-trim change on weapons release. Judging by Indian MiG-27s, the glove pylons can be fitted with beams that allow each to carry two bombs in tandem. The MiG-27 is also capable of carrying the AS-7 *Kerry*, AS-10 *Karen*,

AS-12 *Kegler* and AS-14 *Kedge* air-to-surface missiles.

The first production MiG-27 was designated *Flogger D*, and is characterized by a sensor 'bullet' at the top of either glove pylon. From 1981 a second version was introduced, designated *Flogger J*, with a revised nose tip, and without the sensor bullets and external armour. This version has a distinctive chine running from the glove root to the intake lip, possibly to improve directional stability. Gunpods can be mounted on the glove pylons, and there are reportedly provisions for the cannon to be depressed in strafing attacks. This aircraft is also being built under licence by Hindustan Aeronautics as the MiG-27M *Bahadur* (Valiant).

The R-29BS-300 engine has a thrust of 25,350 lb (11,500 kg), but the pitot intakes of the MiG-27 are believed to restrict speed to Mach 1.7 at altitude, though the low level figure of Mach 1.1 is unchanged. From Indian sources, clean gross weight is 34,170 lb (15,500 kg), and maximum take-off weight is 44,312 lb (20,100 kg) with six 1100 lb (500 kg) bombs and two 176 Imp gal (800 litre) droptanks. For this configuration *SMP-87* gives a 325 nm (600 km) HI-LO-LO-HI radius. At time of writing the SAF is thought to be operating around 800 MiG-27s.

Further Fitters

The array of new Soviet aircraft exhibited in 1967 included two relatively crude technology demonstrators. One was the MiG-21DPD *Fishbed G* with two lift engines in the centre fuselage, a project that immediately sank without trace. The other was the Su-7IG *Fitter B*, which had first flown on 2 August 1966, and (despite its unpromising appearance) was to provide the basis

Libyan markings comprising a green rectangle on the fin and roundels on the wings are carried on this Su-22M-2 *Fitter J*. The outer wing pylons carry 600 litre fuel tanks, while the missiles are *Atolls*. (*US Navy*)

Undercarriage and flaps down, wings fully forward, undernose landing lights on and quadruple airbrakes extended—a Soviet Frontal Aviation Su-17 comes into land. Even before touchdown, the pilot will probably deploy the brakechute from the bullet fairing at the base of the fin.
(*US Navy*)

for a ground attack series produced in large numbers.

As noted earlier, the fixed-wing Su-7B had entered service around 1960. It was a rugged aircraft of useful size, but its fuel capacity was very limited, and its highly swept wing was heavy and far from conducive to short field performance. In the same way that Area Rule saved the Convair F-102, the swing-wing saved the Su-7.

At first sight the Su-7 was not a good subject for variable-geometry conversion, since its main undercarriage units were not only wing-mounted, but quite wide in track. This dictated wing hinges much further outboard than the optimum NASA solution, implying less aero-dynamic benefits and perhaps a larger AC move-ment with wing sweep variation. That the resulting Su-17/20/22 series has acceptable handling

characteristics without resort to FBW controls is presumably due to such a small percentage of the wing moving that AC shift is minimal. A figure of 2 per cent chord has been stated by Soviet sources. By the same token, the weight penalty of the hinges and operating mechanism is probably not excessive. The surprise is really that the improvement in airfield performance warranted the switch to the swing-wing.

The first production series was the Su-17 *Fitter C*, which differed from the prototype mainly in having the 15 per cent more powerful 24,700 lb (11,200 kg) Lyulka AL-21F-3 in place of the AL-7F-1. The principal external difference was the introduction of a wing fence on the glove,

Sukhoi extensively modified an Su-7 airframe to produce a technology demonstrator for the Su-17 series of attack aircraft. It was designated Su-7IG, was brightly painted and first appeared at the 1967 Domodedovo display.

A camouflaged *Fitter H* equipped for reconnaissance with a large multi-sensor pod under the fuselage containing optical, infrared and radar-based equipment.

supplementing the action of the massive fence at the hinge. The *Fitter C* entered service in 1971, and has been used in small numbers by Tactical Aviation and Naval Aviation. For export to Algeria, Czechoslovakia, Egypt, Iraq, Poland and Vietnam, this aircraft is designated Su-20, and has a reduced equipment standard.

In the mid-1970s the Su-17M *Fitter D* introduced a slightly stretched front fuselage, with provisions for a laser ranger in the intake centrebody, and a ventral fairing housing a Doppler radar. For export (Peru being the first customer) this became the Su-22 *Fitter F*, with a modified avionics fairing, an enlarged dorsal fin extension, and the 25,350 lb (11,500 kg) Tumansky R-29BS-300 used in the MiG-27, this engine being associated with a bulged rear fuselage.

The SAF employs a two seat trainer known as

A well-used Su-17 *Fitter H* of a Soviet unit. This is a later series aircraft with the additional missile rail between the two existing wing pylons and upgraded avionics.

---

the Su-17UM *Fitter E*, in which the avionics fairing and the left-hand cannon are deleted, the spine is enlarged to increase fuel volume, and the dorsal fin extension is enlarged.

The next single-seater for the SAF was *Fitter H*, with an enlarged fairing behind the canopy, and the lower front fuselage lines revised to allow the Doppler radar to be housed internally. This variant also introduced two additional wing pylons on the wing gloves. The vertical tail is increased in height, and the aircraft is sometimes fitted with a strake under the rear fuselage, probably associated with certain load configurations.

The *Fitter H* forms the basis for the Tumansky-engined export Su-22 *Fitter J*, which is distinguished by a modified dorsal fin and lacks the extra glove pylons. Another derivative of *Fitter H* is the two-seat Su-22U *Fitter G*, which has an operational capability, and has also been built in Tumansky-engined form.

The final production single-seater is believed to be the *Fitter K*, which appeared in 1984 and has a distinctive intake at the front end of the dorsal fin. As exported to Czechoslovakia, East

Germany and Poland, this aircraft is designated Su-22M-4. A 'Wild Weasel' version reportedly has provisions for the AS-12 *Kegler* anti-radar missile.

It is believed that around 1000 Su-17s are currently operated by the SAF, and a small number of Naval Aviation. The empty weight for a late-production Su-17 is probably in the region of 21,000 lb (9520 kg), implying a clean gross weight of about 30,000 lb (13,600 kg) and a maximum of perhaps 39,000 lb (17,700 kg) with an external load of 8500 lb (3850 kg). The Su-17 retains the two root-mounted 30 mm guns of the Su-7, and has four pylons under the fuselage, two under the massive kink-fence, and (in the case of *Fitter H/J*) four under the wing gloves. These glove pylons are ahead of the CG and may be

restricted to lighter loads such as the K-13 (AA-2 *Atoll*) and AS-7 *Kerry* missiles, and 57/80 mm rocket pods. Recent photographs have shown Warsaw Pact Su-17/22s equipped with upward-firing linear chaff/flare dispensers mounted beside the spine on the centre and rear fuselage.

The *Fitter D/H* aircraft is credited in *SMP-87* with a maximum speed of Mach 2.1 and a HI-LO-LO-HI radius of 300 nm (550 km) with 6600 lb (3000 kg) of ordnance plus external fuel. This radius figure may be an overestimate, as it is only marginally less than that for the MiG-27 *Flogger D/J*, which clearly has far more internal fuel.

Fencer

The most important strike fighter in the Soviet inventory is the Su-24 *Fencer* (bureau designation T-6). This aircraft is generally regarded as having been inspired by the swing-wing F-111, but in reality it may owe just as much in terms of origin to Britain's ill-fated, fixed-wing TSR.2.

From the late 1950s most West European air forces were convinced that deep penetrations of

---

Three early variants of the Su-17/20/22 series known to NATO as *Fitter D*, *Fitter F* (note the changed dorsal spine shape) and *Fitter E*. (*Pilot Press*)

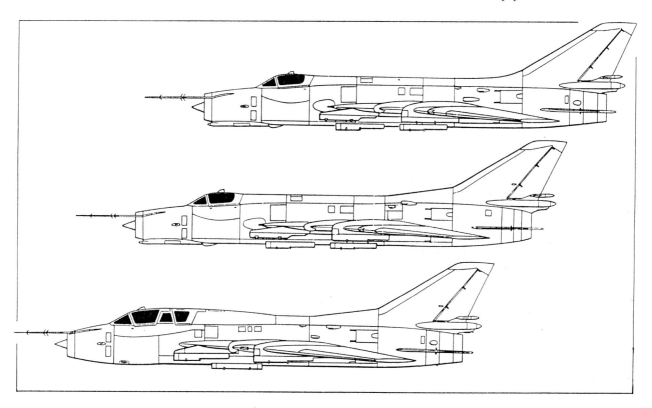

This *Fencer C* version of the Su-24, like others in V-VS service is finished in blue-grey upper surfaces, light blue undersides with a light grey radome. The individual aircraft number is applied to the sides of the intakes and a winged marking, associated with Sukhoi, is often painted below the cockpit as seen in the previous picture.

enemy territory would be possible only by means of high-speed low level flight, which in turn would demand comparatively heavy aircraft, due to the associated high fuel consumption. The principal project to result was the BAC TSR.2, powered by two Olympus engines, each providing up to 30,610 lb (13,880 kg) of static thrust. Its maximum weight was 105,000 lb (47,620 kg), allowing it to carry a 2000 lb (900 kg) nuclear store over a HI-LO-LO-HI radius of 1000 nm (1850 km). Some 10 per cent of that radius was to be flown at Mach 1.7 at altitude, and 20 per cent at Mach 0.9 at low level. Alternatively, it offered a LO-LO radius of 700 nm (1286 km). The TSR.2 first flew on 27 September 1964 (ie, three months before the F-111), but it was terminated as an economy measure in April 1965.

It is known that a fixed wing was also employed for the first prototype of the Su-24, which is now exhibited at Monino. Its first flight date has not yet been published, but it must have been around 1965. It seems quite likely that (as was certainly true for the TSR.2) it had grown considerably in weight since it was first conceived, and that its airfield requirement had consequently extended far beyond the planned figure. In any event, the Su-24 was redesigned to make use of a swing-wing, the new prototype taking to the air around 1970, doubtless helped by the Sukhoi bureau's experience with the Su-7IG and Su-17. It may be noted that the engineer in charge of Su-24 operational development and testing was Simonov, who was to become chief designer for the Su-27.

The *Fencer A* entered service at the end of 1974, replacing the Yak-28 *Brewer*. However, deployments outside the Soviet Union did not take place until 1979, when some were temporarily based at Templin near Berlin. The type was clearly regarded as providing a quantum leap in strike capability, and thus in need of special security measures and restrictions on overseas sales. In fact, exports of the Su-24 were not to begin until it had been in service for 15 years, and to date only three countries have received it.

The Su-24 might be regarded as having a

Lack of hard information as to the true role of the Su-24, prompted NATO analysts in 1974 to allocate the name *Fencer* to the new aircraft. It soon became known that the Su-24 was a low-level bomber which should have received a name in the B-series. However, *Fencer* was retained and remains the only major anomaly among the current list of Soviet reporting or code-names. Shown is a *Fencer D +* .

variable-sweep wing of the NASA type, probably because it was not constrained by undercarriage considerations, and could thus be optimized for aerodynamic benefits. Sweep is reportedly selected by the pilot, who chooses a leading edge angle of 16°, 45°, or 68° according to Mach No. Like the F-111, the Su-24 has side-by-side seating, and there have been suggestions that the Sukhoi cockpit is somewhat cramped. The undercarriage is fuselage-mounted, the main gears retracting forwards. All three units have twin wheels, indicating design emphasis on operation from badly-surfaced runways. It may be noted that the TSR.2 was supposed to be operable from grass, and (like the Viggen) it had tandem mainwheels, which reduce drag on soft surfaces.

Relative to the F-111, the Su-24 is raised much higher off the ground, allowing large stores to be carried under the fuselage. The Su-24 has four belly-mounted pylons, plus two under the wing gloves and two variable-sweep pylons under the outer wings. When the type made its public debut at Frunze in August 1989 in the form of an Su-24MK *Fencer D*, it was carrying an AS-11 *Kilter* anti-radiation missile on the centreline station. It is also assumed to be capable of carrying the AS-10 *Karen*, AS-12 *Kegler*, AS-13 and AS-14 *Kedge*.

On either side of the forward centreline pylon is a large bulge, the one on the right evidently housing a 30 mm Gatling-type gun, though the purpose of the left-hand excrescence is not clear. The aircraft has two (MiG-like) ventral airbrakes, which are formed in part by the surfaces of these fairings.

The day/night all-weather equipment fit of the Su-24 presumably includes Doppler-inertial navigation (bearing in mind the aircraft's age and long radius of action), plus a terrain-following radar, head-up display and laser ranging. One senior US Army officer is reported to have said that it can deliver ordnance within 180 ft (55 m) of its target regardless of weather conditions.

The initial production variant, *Fencer A*, was distinguished by a rectangular-section rear-end that completely enclosed the afterburner nozzles.

A fine view of an early *Fencer C*. This version has largely been supplanted in Soviet service by *Fencer D*, identified by the longer nose. It is worth noting that the Su-24 was the first Soviet aircraft with pivoting pylons.

The aim was presumably to provide flat surfaces on which the tailplane could rotate, to optimize effectiveness and reduce drag. Cooling air from the engine bays would be vented into the gaps around the nozzles to reduce base drag.

The rear-end has subsequently gone through several stages of refinement, beginning with *Fencer B*, in which the underside of the rear fuselage is channelled out between the jetpipes. It also has a larger fairing for the braking parachute, which is mounted at the base of the vertical tail.

The third production model (*Fencer C*) entered service in 1981, but the first good photographs appeared only three years later, when it was encountered by Swedish aircraft over the Baltic. It is identified by a large number of sensors around the front fuselage, and by the rear fuselage being cut back to reveal the afterburner nozzles. It later appears to have grown a small fairing ahead of the wing glove root, possibly housing an RWR sensor.

The *Fencer D* entered service in 1984, and has large fences over enlarged glove pylons, which are possibly associated with the AS-14 missile. It also has an unusual leading edge extension of the lower fin, and a lengthened nose carrying a long probe. In this case the rear fuselage covers the nozzles. This variant has a retractable probe for in-flight refuelling (mounted just ahead of the windscreen) and a large EO blister just behind the nose undercarriage.

Fencer E is believed to be a reconnaissance version of *Fencer D*. This variant is also used by Naval Aviation, which began replacing Tu-16s of

the Baltic Fleet with these aircraft in 1985. It presumably differs in terms of sensor fit, and is distinguished by side-looking windows behind the nosewheel bay. An electronic warfare Su-24 is now in service and will probably replace the Yak-28 *Brewer E.* It may be expected to be given the designation *Fencer F.*

It is estimated that over 800 Su-24s are now serving with the SAF in the interdiction and strike roles, and that approximately 65 are assigned to reconnaissance duties with the SAF and Naval Aviation.

Exports of the Su-24 began in March 1989 when six were carried in An-22 transports from Novosibirsk to Libya's Umm Aitiquah airfield. It is felt that (although the Soviets have provided assurances that these aircraft do not have flight refuelling provisions) they may at some stage pose a threat to US Navy units in the Mediterranean and (if moved to Bumbah, near Tobruk) to Israeli targets.

Three-view of an electronic warfare version of the Su-24, identified by the blade aerial under the nose, which may receive the designator *Fencer F.* (***Pilot Press***)

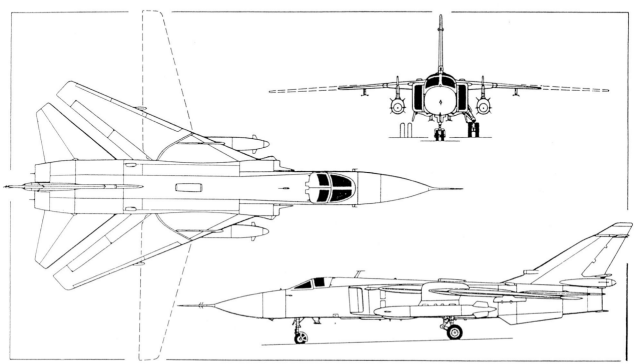

Israeli sources have also claimed that Iraq has 15 *Fencer C*s, and that deliveries to Syria were 'imminent', although neither report has been confirmed by US intelligence. Other sources indicate that Syria signed a contract for Su-24s in late 1987 but failed to make progress payments. It is considered possible that Libya may provide financial support for this purchase.

Despite these exports, no details of the Su-24 have as yet been published by the Soviet Union. This aircraft clearly needs a great deal of fuel to achieve a useful range, but it is generally assumed to be equipped with two very powerful 24,700 lb (11,200 kg) Lyulka AL-21F-3 turbojets, as used in the Su-17 series, although R-29 turbofans would appear more logical.

By comparison with the F-111, it may be estimated that the Su-24 has an empty weight of around 41,000 lb (18,600 kg), a clean take-off weight of approximately 75,000 lb (34,000 kg) and a maximum in the region of 90,000 lb (40,800 kg). According to *SMP-87*, the Su-24 has a maximum speed of Mach 2.0, and a HI-LO-LO-HI radius of 700 nm (1300 km) with a 6600 lb (3000 kg) of ordnance, using external fuel.

To put the Su-24 into perspective, it is much larger (and over 30 per cent heavier) than the Tornado IDS, and only slightly lighter than the F-111A. The latter appears to be marginally superior in maximum speed and warload-radius performance, but the Su-24 has a much higher thrust/weight ratio. It is thus likely to be especially superior in terms of penetration speed without afterburner. The Su-24 also has some capability to operate from unpaved runways. Perhaps more significantly, it has the performance to pose a potential threat to vital air lines of communication across the North Atlantic, though there is as yet no sign of the equipment and armament needed to perform the long-range intercept role.

Backfire

Returning to the subject of bombers, the preceding chapter outlined the development of the Tu-22 *Blinder* as the planned supersonic successor to the Tu-16 in the intermediate range bombing and maritime strike roles. Although this new aircraft did provide a limited (Mach 1.4) supersonic dash capability, the Soviets evidently felt that too high a price had been paid in terms of radius of action. Procurement of the Tu-22 was consequently limited, while the development of an improved design was launched.

The Tu-22M alias *Backfire C*, latest version of this bomber and maritime reconnaissance/attack aircraft. Differing from *Backfire B* in having wedge-shaped engine intakes, this particular Naval-operated example carries an external stores rack in addition to the large underwing weapon pylons for *Kitchen* (AS-4) ASMs.

In essence, the resulting Tu-22M *Backfire* is a significantly heavier aircraft than the Tu-22, with more powerful engines that are housed within the rear fuselage, rather than mounted above it. The Tu-22M also features Phantom-or Vigilante-style intakes and a cleaner undercarriage installation. It nonetheless seems to have begun life as an extensively redesigned Tu-22, hence the Tu-22M designation used by President Brezhnev in his 1979 statement aimed at excluding this aircraft from the SALT-2 talks.

It is thought that development began around 1965, ie, four years after the Tu-22 entered service. Most of the fuselage was completely new, but the prototypes (at least) may well have made use of some nose, wing, tail and undercarriage components from the Tu-22 production line. On the pre-series *Backfire A*, the main undercarriage bogies certainly retracted aft into trailing edge fairings, similar to those of the Tu-22.

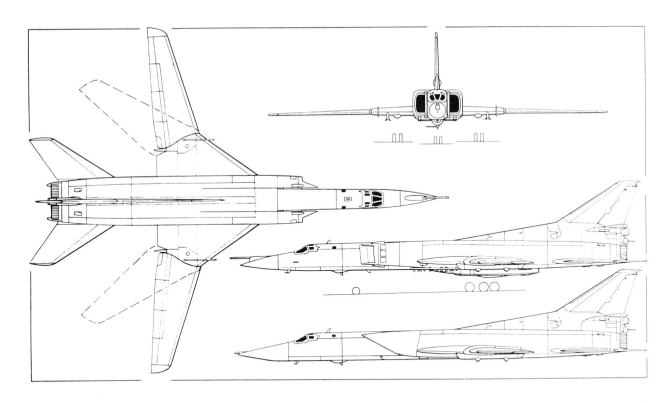

LEFT **Three-view of Tu-22M *Backfire B* armed with a Kitchen ASM and a comparison side-view of *Backfire C*. (*Pilot Press*)**

BOTTOM LEFT **To date, *Backfire* has not been exported outside the USSR, and the aircraft remains a formidable long-range strike aircraft, with or without its controversial refuelling probe and plumbing!**

As in the case of the Su-17, the development of a swing-wing derivative from an existing aircraft equipped with a wing-mounted main undercarriage severely restricted the amount of wing that could be swung. Nonetheless, contrary to Western design philosophy, worthwhile improvements in subsonic cruise performance and reductions in airfield demands could evidently still be obtained, in combination with a reduced weight penalty and an acceptable AC shift.

The Soviets have never disclosed the type of engines fitted to the Tu-22M, but it is generally assumed to have a pair of Kuznetsov NK-144 turbofans similar to the four employed in the now-defunct Tu-144 SST. The civil rating for the NK-144 was approximately 44,100 lb (20,000 kg).

Following the manufacture of the preseries batch, construction switched around 1975 to *Backfire B*, which some Western observers suspect was redesignated Tu-26, rather than Tu-22M. This first main production version introduced a wing of much larger span, and main undercarriage units that retract inboard, so that the wheels are housed in the outer sections of the very wide fuselage, thus avoiding the drag of the earlier trailing edge fairings. It has two GSh-23 cannon in a radar-directed tail barbette.

The aircraft has a crew of four. *Backfire B* is normally seen with a flight refuelling probe mounted above the nose radome, although dur-

Aircraft number '42' is a *Backfire B*. Some aircraft appear to carry no individual identification, but the number is almost always painted on the nosewheel doors as an aid to ground maintenance operations. This Soviet Naval Aviation Tu-22M has the standard dark grey/light grey colour scheme and carries an earlier type of external multiple-store rack.

ing the SALT-2 treaty negotiations the probe was removed, apparently to support Soviet claims that the 'Tu-22M' is purely a medium-range bomber with no intercontinental capability. Brezhnev's 1979 statement that there was no intention for the aircraft to employ flight refuelling was widely taken as a bare-faced lie, but the real point may have been that the SAF regards refuelling *Backfire* in flight as an emergency means of extending time on station, rather than a routine way to extend radius.

The third version (*Backfire C*) appeared in prototype form in the late 1970s. It differs from its predecessors in having Vigilante-type intakes, a slightly upturned radome for its *Down-Beat* nose-radar, and a single GSh-23 in the tail turret (below the *Bee-Hind* radar that directs it). In this variant there appears to be no fixed refuelling probe, though a retracting probe is possible.

Backfire is estimated to have a maximum weight of almost 300,000 lb (136,000 kg), making it 50 per cent heavier than the Tu-22 and 80 per cent heavier than the Tu-16. In *SMP-87* it is credited with a Mach 2.0 dash capability and an unrefuelled radius of 2150 nm (4000 km), compared to 1670 nm (3100 km) for the Tu-16 and 1565 nm (2900 km) for the Tu-22. The type originally carried a single AS-4 *Kitchen* semi-recessed on the centreline, but launching shoes for this missile are now mounted on either glove pylon, roughly in line with the hinge. It is estimated that bombs up to a total of 26,460 lb (12,000 kg) may be carried internally.

There are believed to be around 400 *Backfire B/Cs* in service, of which over one third are with Naval Aviation. Brezhnev's 1979 statement included an assurance that there was no intention to increase the production rate above the then-current 30 per year, and there is no evidence that this rate has been exceeded.

Although a *Backfire* with flight refuelling could in principle pose a threat to North America, it is seen primarily as menacing Western Europe, China, and various maritime areas. Its combination of a useful radius, a heavy warload, and a supersonic low level penetration capability make it a very serious opponent. Perhaps surprisingly, *Backfire* is not expected to serve as a platform for the AS-15 cruise missile.

Close Support

In the late 1960s, presumably encouraged by Britain's success with jet-lift aircraft, some Soviet designers were instructed to study the possibility of a fixed-wing VTOL close support aircraft that could function like a high-speed helicopter and could live with front-line units of the Red Army.

They therefore looked for a powerplant system that would permit VTOL from natural surfaces unprotected by metal planking. In essence, the only way to achieve such capability is to use the propulsion engines to drive lifting fans. Ideally, these fans should be vectorable and retractable, and they would thus be heavy and costly. The Soviets presumably reached some such conclusion, and abandoned the exercise.

The Soviet VTOL close support programme survived only in the context of a Naval Aviation aircraft, primarily intended to cover amphibious landing operations. The Red Army's close support requirements were ultimately met by the combination of an attack helicopter and a fixed-wing aircraft that achieved short field performance by virtue of low wing loading. Both concepts have some good features, but they are clearly more vulnerable to ground fire and interception by enemy fighters than the much faster V/STOL Harrier series operated by the RAF and USMC. This writer would argue that the Soviets misjudged the potential of jet lift aircraft, because they demanded pure VTOL (which kills disposable load and maximizes ground erosion) and rejected the use of aluminium planking (which is a minor logistics problem in army terms).

Forger

The first public manifestation of Soviet V/STOL developments occurred in 1967, when two examples of the twin-engined Yak-36 *Freehand* technology demonstrator were shown at Domodedovo, one statically and one in flight. The Yak-36 was effectively a large, rehashed Bell X-14, the only significant difference being that the Yakovlev powerplant employed rotatable nozzles, whereas the X-14 used two sets of 45°

Hardly in the same league as the Hawker P.1127, the Yak-36 *Freehand* caused quite a stir when it made its one and only public appearance at the 1967 Domodedovo display. Two of these small VTOL experimental aircraft were shown and were to pave the way for the later Yak-38.

turning vanes behind each engine, one fixed and one rotatable.

The X-14, which first hovered on 19 February 1957 and made its first transitions on 24 May 1958, was the first V/STOL research aircraft of real significance, but its direct development potential was very limited. Since they were to supply jet lift under the CG, the engines had to be placed well forward, and their weight could be balanced only by placing the pilot well aft. A conventional high-speed aircraft configuration, with pilot and radar in the nose, was therefore impossible.

The Bell aircraft had started out with two 1750 lb (795 kg) Viper engines, and later switched to 2450 lb (1110 kg) J85s, but the

Yak-36 probably had two Koliesov engines of 7875 lb (3570 kg) thrust. It was evident from TV film taken in 1967 that the Yak-36 had a very positive thrust margin and was strongly auto-stabilized. No Harrier ever shot off the ground like the Yak-36, or was as rock-steady at the hover.

There were reports of the Yak-36 carrying out sea trials on board the half-deck cruiser *Moskva*, but then no further word of Soviet V/STOL

OVERLEAF Each of the four *Kiev* class carrier/cruisers accommodates 12 Yak-38 V/STOL combat aircraft plus two two-seat trainer versions. NATO designate them *Forger A* and *B* respectively. INSET LEFT This example is being spotted on the flight deck and has the door to its two lift engines open as well as the exhaust doors under the forward fuselage. INSET RIGHT Long approaches to the carrier deck are a feature of *Forger* operations, the aircraft crossing the stern at around 5 knots (9 km/hr) before hovering and descending vertically. All aircraft carry the Soviet Navy flag marking together with the individual aircraft number on each side behind the engine intake.
(*US Navy*)

During early operations, *Forgers* were noted taking off vertically with a gradual transition to forward flight. This technique was superseded by a STOL take-off which gave the aircraft a better payload/range capability.
(*TASS*)

developments until 1975, when a completely new aircraft was seen operating VTOL from the equally new 40,000 ton helicopter carrier *Kiev*, during its trials in the Black Sea.

On 12 July 1976 this ship passed through the Bosphorus and entered the Mediterranean, and its fixed-wing complement was declared to be Yak-36 aircraft. More recently it has become accepted that the normal complement for each of the four ships of this class (*Kiev*, *Minsk*, *Novorossiyk* and *Baku*) is 12 single-seaters and one two-seater.

It was originally thought in the West that the full designation for this new aircraft was Yak-36MP, but in 1984 the Polish magazine *Morze* referred to it as the Yak-38, and this was subsequently accepted by most West publications. For reporting purposes the single-seater is known to NATO as *Forger A*, and the two-seater as *Forger B*.

The powerplant concept might be regarded as a derivative of that of the X-14, or as a rehash of Germany's VFW1262. Whereas the X-14 (and Yak-36 copy) used two engines side-by-side, to cancel out lateral thrust components as the nozzles rotated, the Yak-38 has a single propulsion engine feeding two rotatable nozzles. To add more jet-lift for take-off and landing, and to move the overall powerplant CG further aft (relative to aircraft CG), two lift engines are located just behind the cockpit.

Compared to the single-engined Harrier, this powerplant arrangement is less safe, since there are more engines to fail, and a large pitching moment in such an emergency. Not surprisingly, *Forger* has an automatic system to monitor aircraft behaviour at low speeds and (if necessary) eject the pilot. This electronic system is known by the Russian abbreviation *Eskem*.

When this picture appeared in 1983, it was the first to show *Forger* armed with AAMs. The missiles are *Aphids* (AA-8), but of equal interest is the glimpse of the two Koliesov lift engines behind the cockpits.

At low speeds the door over the lift engines is opened, and provides additional air via spring-loaded louvres. Unlike some earlier Western lift-engined projects, there are no side-plates to this door, hence in approaching to land it cannot provide ram air to start the lift engines. The implication is probably that the two lift engines are started with bleed air from the main engine. In the course of development, strakes have been added alongside this door and extending further aft, to reduce the recirculation of hot gases, and perhaps also to improve directional stability.

Initial operations used only VTOL, but rolling VTOs were employed later, probably to reduce recirculation and deck-heating, rather than to benefit wing-lift. Like its predecessor, the Yak-38 appears to have a high-authority autostabilizer, as its low-speed flight is rock-steady. Its reaction control system differs from that of the Harrier family in that there is no pitch control in the nose, a change that reduces intake problems associated with hot gases and FOD. It is, of course, possible that low-speed pitch control is provided by differential throttle. The Yakovlev aircraft also differs in having a conventional undercarriage. Its track is much narrower than the outriggers of the Harrier, and this clearly facilitates manoeuvr-

ing close to the deck edge. Its wings fold, reducing span to approximately 16 ft (4.9 m), and allowing it to use carrier lifts designed for helicopters. However, *Forger B* is a very long aircraft at around 60 ft (18.3 m).

Aside from a small IRST sensor just ahead of the windscreen, there is little evidence of operational equipment. This suggests that the Yak-38 is basically a technology demonstrator, a conclusion that is supported by the fact that this aircraft was not offered to the Indian Navy as an alternative to the Sea Harrier. *Forger* is normally equipped with four underwing pylons, though often only the outer pair are used. Typical stores are the AA-8 *Aphid*, AS-7 *Kerry*, the 57 mm rocket pod, and a 23 mm gunpod.

Based largely on the amount of smoke emitted by the propulsion engine, it was initially believed in the West to be a Lyulka AL-21 turbojet, a non-afterburning variant of that used in the Su-17. However, a TsIAM exhibition in Moscow in early 1990 included the actual engine: the Tumansky (some reports say Mukulin/Soyuz) R27V-300, a 15,300 lb (6940 kg) engine weighing 2980 lb (1350 kg). The R-27 is a two-shaft engine with five low-pressure and six high-pressure compressor stages, each driven by a single turbine stage. The two thrust-vectoring nozzles are rotated by hydraulic motors, with a transverse shaft to ensure symmetric operation.

The same exhibition included sectioned example of the Koliesov (some reports say Rybinsk) 7875 lb (3570 kg) RD-36-35FVR lift engine, two of which combine with the R-27 to give a nominal lifting force of 31,050 lb (14,080 kg). On this basis, *Forger* was probably designed for a VTO weight of around 23,150 lb (10,500 kg) in quite high ambient temperatures. Assuming an empty weight of 15,000 lb (6800 kg), the Yak-38 probably has 4400 lb (200 kg) of internal fuel, and can carry external stores in the region of 3000 lb (1360 kg).

Foreshortened view of *Kiev*'s 620 ft (189 m)-long flight deck which is angled at $4\frac{1}{2}°$. Behind the four Kamov Ka-25 Hormone ASW helicopters is a scorched area of deck indicating the *Forger* operating area; two of these aircraft are on the right.

These figures suggest a LO-LO attack radius of about 100 nm (185 km) and a HI-LO-LO-HI radius of perhaps 180 nm (335 km). In a CAP mission, it can probably remain on station for almost an hour at 100 nm (185 km) radius. Maximum reconnaissance radius is probably 250 nm (460 km). Reports suggest that the Yak-38 has been tracked on radar while flying at Mach 1.05 at altitude.

To summarize, although *Forger* has far more thrust than a Sea Harrier, it is also a much heavier aircraft, due to its three engines. In consequence, its performance is not really impressive, though it may be marginally transonic at altitude. *Forger* also presents additional engineering problems, since it requires more servicing and maintenance manpower, and increased spares storage. Its uses are probably restricted to close support for amphibious landings, daylight clear weather air defence, and reconnaissance.

Attack Helicopters

In the late 1960s the Soviets appear to have concluded after several years of configuration studies that fixed-wing V/STOL aircraft could not provide a practical solution to their future close support needs in the context of the land battle. Looking at Britain's Pegasus-powered Harrier, they may well have decided that it represented an expensive development, yet gave only limited warload-radius capability from VTOL. The Harrier was also not really compatible with VTOL from natural surfaces on a year-round basis, which was the desired Red Army concept.

The USAF was meanwhile showing no interest in V/STOL, but was at that time planning a turboprop STOL aircraft for the COIN war in South Vietnam. Such an aircraft would have no possible application in Europe, but the US Army's armed helicopters were proving a great success in Vietnam, and such aircraft might have a valuable role to play on the Central Front.

America is generally credited with having pioneered the armed helicopter concept, but the Soviet Union has not been slow to apply weapons

to rotary-wing aircraft. Their main initial development (perhaps encouraged by US experience in SE Asia) was to apply rocket pods to their vast number of assault helicopters, to blanket the landing zone with suppressive fire.

The Mi-8 *Hip C* thus has four hardpoints, each capable of carrying a 32-round 57 mm rocket pod (the UV-32-57). In the assault helicopter context, this was followed by the *Hip E*, which remains the most heavily armed helicopter in the world. It has a flexibly-mounted 12.7 mm machine gun in the nose, and mounting points for six UV-32-57 rocket pods in addition to four AT-2 *Swatter* missiles. The Mi-17 *Hip H* is the first of the series to carry cannon for fire suppression, using the twin-barrel 23 mm GSh-23 in podded form.

In addition to these stores, the Mi-8/17 series (the Mi-17 differing primarily in having more powerful engines) has up to 24 seats in the cabin, though a normal load is probably 12–14 fully-armed troops. As a front-line target *Hip* is comparatively large, and has always been considered vulnerable to ground fire, especially from the sides. The Mi-17 therefore has external armour plate in the cockpit area, and the Mi-8MT exhibited at Frunze in August 1989 had similar armour plus three 32-round chaff/flare dispensers on either side, adjacent to the engine exhausts.

Over 10,000 of the *Hip* series have been built, and around a quarter of these still serve with the Soviet forces. The series has also been supplied to the forces of about 40 other nations.

To complement the *Hip*, it was decided to develop a somewhat smaller helicopter with more speed and manoeuvrability, retaining cabin space for up to eight fully armed troops, but with more capability in the attack role. The result is officially described as a 'combat transport helicopter', and is designated Mi-24 or *Hind*.

A short-cut to producing an attack helicopter quickly is to use as many existing components as possible. Mil did this using items from his Mi-8 *Hip* series. The result was the Mi-24, seen here in initial *Hind A* form armed with four UB-32 rocket pods and four *Swatter* (AT-2) ATGW launch rails.

ABOVE Prompted by operations in Afghanistan where the 12.7 mm Gatling machine-gun of *Hind D* and *E* was deficient in range and hitting power, a twin-barrel 30 mm cannon rectified these shortcomings and resulted in the *Hind F* designator. Below the gun muzzles is a low-light TV sensor housing. (*Roy Braybrook*)

TOP RIGHT Tail view of *Hind F* which has the export designation Mil Mi-35. Interestingly, the stub wings which can carry a range of weaponry also provide some 25 per cent of the total lift in cruising flight. The wing endplate pylons carry *Spiral* (AT-6) tube-launched anti-armour missiles. (*Roy Braybrook*)

RIGHT In the early seventies, the Mi-24 underwent a significant redesign which produced the sinister-looking *Hind D* with its distinctive stepped cockpits for gunner (front) and pilot (rear). *Hind E* and *F* (seen here) followed, each variant increasing the type's attack capability. (*Barry Wheeler*)

Close-up of the three UB-32 rocket pods and three *Sagger* (AT-3) ATGW mounts which, with a similar load on the right-hand side and a 12.7 mm MG in the nose, form the armament of the Mi-8 *Hip F* assault helicopter. This is the export variant of the Soviet-operated *Hip E*.

Preliminary work on this project appears to have begun in the early 1960s, long before the death of the bureau's chief designer Mikhail L Mil on 31 January 1970. Marat N Tischenko then took over that role, with Alexei Ivanov as his deputy. First flight of the Mi-24 is said by Aviaexport officials to have occurred 'about 1970'.

Like the *Hip* series, the Mi-24 has a five-blade main rotor and a three-blade tail rotor. Power was initially provided by two Isotov (Leningrad bureau) TV2s of 1500 shp, but these were replaced by TV3-117s of 1950 shp, with a 2200 shp contingency rating. However, the blade design was new, and (unlike *Hip*) the Mi-24 has a retractable undercarriage. The Mi-24 began life with a single cockpit, in which two pilots sat side-by-side, with a weapons operator in the nose to control the single 12.7 mm machine gun.

The *Hind A* designation was applied to both the TV2-engined aircraft with the tail rotor on the right, and the TV3 version with the tail rotor on the left. Steeply-drooped auxiliary wings carried four weapons pylons and wingtip mountings for a total of four AT-2s. *Hind* is also believed to be capable of mounting UPK-23 gunpods, up to 3300 lb (1500 kg) of bombs, and PFM-1 minelet-dispensers. There are provisions

An unusual fixed and rotary-wing formation seen at the Moscow air show in 1989. An Mi-24 *Hind F* trundles past with two Sukhoi Su-27 *Flanker Bs* showing a commendable degree of stability at low speed despite the downwash from the helicopter's rotor blades.

for firing assault rifles from the cabin windows. *Hind A* entered service in late 1973 or early 1974. Airframe life is 2000 hr, with overhauls at 200 hr intervals.

The project then underwent a role-change, with the attack mission given far higher priority. To improve effectiveness in the gunship role (in which it has both an air-to-ground and an air-to-air capability), the flight deck was completely reconfigured, to produce two cockpits in tandem. In essence, the copilot was removed, the pilot was relocated on the centreline, and the gunner was placed in a separate front cockpit, carrying out the roles of observer/gunner and emergency pilot.

The single-barrel DShK machine gun was meanwhile replaced by a four-barrel 12.7 mm Gatling-type gun, mounted in a chin turret. The new production standard was designated *Hind D*, and it entered service in 1975. Reports suggest that the export designation is Mi-25. It is also believed that *Hind D* was the 'A-10' helicopter

that in September 1978 established a speed record of 198.9 knots (368.4 km/hr) over a 25 km course.

The next variant was *Hind E*, modified to permit a total of up to eight AT-6s to be carried. Guidance for this radar beam-riding missile is provided from a radome mounted under the left side of the nose. An Iraqi *Hind* is believed to have shot down an Iranian F-4 during the Gulf War, using an AT-6. The four underwing pylons may be used to carry the AA-2 *Atoll* or AA-8 *Aphid* missiles for air-to-air combat.

The generally similar *Hind F* has a fixed two-barrel 30 mm cannon (GSh-30-2) on the right side of the front fuselage, and the 12.7 mm Gatling is deleted. This variant was developed specifically to out-range ground fire in Afghanistan. The Mi-35 export designation seems to apply to both the *Hind E* and *F*.

Both the pilot and the gunner have flat bulletproof windscreens and double-curvature hoods. The pilot's door is on the right and the gunner's on the left. The pilot has a large weapon-aiming display, while the gunner has a small overhead-mounted reflector sight for rockets and the 30 mm gun, which is fed from a 124/250-round magazine under the rear cockpit floor. He also has an inverted binocular periscopic sight linked to a sight-head under the nose. The gunner has flight instruments, collective- and cyclic-pitch controls, and a rudder bar, so that he can fly the aircraft in emergency. Both cockpits have 6 mm titanium armour and NBC canopy seals, and are separated by an armoured bulkhead. Both also have Doppler/ADC-fed moving map displays.

The Mi-24 series made its Western debut in September 1989, when a *Hind F* with the export designation Mi-35P was presented at Helitech-89 at Redhill in Surrey. It was armed with four 20-round pods (B-8-V20s) for the new 80 mm rockets, which are evidently replacing the 57 mm, and four mockup AT-6 missiles. A similar aircraft exhibited at Frunze in the previous month was designated Mi-24G.

The data-board for this Mi-35P confirmed the use of two 2200 shp TV3-117s, and gave a maximum take-off weight of 25,355 lb (11,500 kg), a maximum level speed of 173 knots (320 km/hr), a hover ceiling of 6560 ft (2000 m) at normal take-off weight, a service ceiling of 14,750 ft (4500 m), and a range of 245 nm (450 km) with 5 per cent reserves. The hover ceiling was evidently in ground effect (IGE).

Other official data subsequently obtained from the Mi-24 brochure included a rotor diameter of 56.75 ft (17.3 m), a tail rotor diameter of 12.82 ft (3.908 m), a wing span of 21.8 ft (6.65 m), and an empty equipped weight of 18,078 lb (8200 kg). Normal take-off weight is given as 24,692 lb (11,200 kg) and maximum weight as 26,455 lb (12,000 kg). Maximum payload is 3310 lb (1500 kg), but maximum external load is given as 5290 lb (2400 kg). The same brochure gives maximum speed as 181 knots (335 km/hr), cruise speed as 145.7 knots (270 km/hr), OGE hover ceiling as 4920 ft (1500 m), and endurance as 4 hr.

It is estimated that around 2500 Mi-24/25/35s have been built, of which roughly half serve with the Red Army. Exports have taken place to Afghanistan, Algeria, Angola, Czechoslovakia, Cuba, East Germany, Hungary, India, Iraq, North Korea, Libya, Mozambique, Nicaragua, Peru, Poland, Vietnam and South Yemen. *Hind B* and *D* (and possibly *E* and *F*) were both used operationally in Afghanistan, and the series has also seen action in Chad, Nicaragua, Angola, Sri Lanka, and the Gulf War. In 1985 two Afghan pilots defected with their Mi-24s to Pakistan, and one of these may well have found its way to America.

Frogfoot

The final combat aircraft of this third postwar generation was the Su-25 (bureau designation T-8) *Frogfoot*, which may be regarded conceptually as the Soviet Union's answer to America's A-10.

The Su-25 was unquestionably inspired by the Fairchild A-10 and Northrop A-9, which competed in the early 1970s for the USAF A-X order. The A-10 first flew on 10 May 1972, and the A-9 exactly 20 days later. The Fairchild aircraft won the contest, with that company's desperate need for work (and Northrop's busy factories) undoubtedly playing some part in the decision.

The Su-25 is in no sense a copy of either of these US designs, but it did follow the general concept of a relatively low speed, highly manoeuvrable and very survivable close support aircraft. In some important respects (notably maximum speed and front-line compatibility, though probably not in cannon effectiveness), the Sukhoi aircraft is distinctly superior.

The Su-25 was not a response to a SAF requirement, but a private venture, promoted initially by the late Pavel Sukhoi (who died in September 1973), in the face of strong opposition from the military. It is described officially as being intended for the close support of ground troops under heavy enemy fire conditions, its principal targets being armoured vehicles, area and point targets, helicopters and low-speed aircraft. The new aircraft had to be highly effective in a first-pass attack, and quick to respond, yet cheap and straightforward to manufacture and simple to operate, demonstrating a high degree of reliability and tolerance of projectile strikes up to 30 mm. It was also to be capable of flying from unpaved airfields with the minimum of preparation, and of operating independently for up to 12 days, using an air-mobile turnround and servicing system carried in pods

This nose view of an Su-25 *Frogfoot* shows the twin-barrel 30 mm cannon at lower right, the laser ranger and marked target seeker window in the centre, strike camera location above and the two probes, the left hand one for instrumentation and the right-hand one being the pitot head. (*Tony Holmes*)

on four of its underwing pylons, and with the Red Army supplying only fuel.

The design engineer in charge of the project was Valdimir P Babak. To avoid the need for significant powerplant development work, it was decided to base the design on a pair of well-established, non-afterburning engines. The initial design therefore employed Tumansky RD-9s from the MiG-19, an approach that clearly resulted in a low-cost aircraft, since the RD-9 produced only 5735 lb (2600 kg) per engine. The result was inevitably a much smaller design than the A-10, since this figure is less than two-thirds the thrust of the TF34 engine.

Powered by two RD-9s, the first Su-25 had its maiden flight on 22 February 1975, almost three years after the A-10. The pilot was Vladimir Ilyushin, son of the designer Sergei Vladimirovich Ilyushin, who died on 9 February 1977 at the age of 82. The first US satellite photographs of the Su-25 were taken over the Ramenskoye test centre in 1977, and the type was given the provisional reporting name *Ram-J*. This was superseded by the designation *Frogfoot* in 1982.

Initial test flights showed that the aircraft was badly underpowered, so it was redesigned around two 8820 lb (4000 kg) Tumansky R-95s, derived from the R-13s of the MiG-21.

The R-95 provided 54 per cent more thrust than the RD-9, and completely transformed the performance of the aircraft. By 1978, two years after the A-10 had entered service, the Sukhoi OKB had finally won a limited degree of military support for the project, and an initial production batch (enough for two trials squadrons) was ordered from the Tbilisi factory.

The Su-25 began coming off the line in 1979, at exactly the right time for the idea of a slow but manoeuvrable close support aircraft to be evaluated operationally against Afghanistan's *mujihadeen* guerillas, who were resisting the

Soviet military occupation. The first two production aircraft arrived in the country before the end of 1980. Two units were eventually formed, attached to the 10th Tactical Air Army. The first was established at Bagram (just north of Kabul) in 1981, and was reported as the 290th Independent Guards Regiment. The second was said to be formed at Shindand in the west of the country toward the end of 1982.

The first poor-quality photographs of the Su-25 flying over Afghanistan were published in the West in late 1982. Reporters operating with the *mujihadeen* said that the Su-25s flew in pairs, one attacking while the other cruised around higher, dispensing flares. They sometimes attacked in conjunction with Mi-24s, their target being marked by smoke or WP rockets fired by other Mi-24s or Mi-8 *Hips*.

Operational evaluation in Afghanistan led to several changes, including the addition of a long-range navigation aid and larger external tanks. Despite the higher thrust of the R-95s, the Su-25 was felt to be still underpowered in hot/high take-offs. The R-95 was therefore replaced on the production line by an uprated derivative (the R-195), giving a 12 per cent increase to 9925 lb (4500 kg).

The introduction of the IR-homing Redeye shoulder-launched SAM in 1984 brought a significant improvement in the guerillas' ability to defend themselves against ground attack aircraft. Two Su-25s were shot down in quick succession, and the aircraft's flare-dispensing capacity was therefore increased from 128 to 256 rounds by the addition of four 32-round strap-on units in tandem pairs over the rear of either engine nacelle. The original fit took the form of upward-firing dispensers mounted within the rear fuselage, on either side of the fin.

In 1986 Redeye was superseded by Stinger, which was far less easily decoyed by flares. Four Su-25s were lost (and two of their pilots were killed) in the first three days. The Sukhoi bureau therefore switched its efforts to minimizing the weapon's terminal effects. Operational research showed that the Stinger's 6.5 lb (2.95 kg) warhead was detonating close to the engine nozzles, with the result that its fragments produced fuel leaks from the rear fuselage tanks. The leaking

---

Fairchild's A-10A Thunderbolt II was probably the inspiration for the Su-25, and like the Soviet aircraft, the American tank-killer has proved itself in battle. Under the port wing of this A-10A is an AN/ALQ-131 ECM pod.
(*Barry Wheeler*)

fuel was then ignited by the hot efflux, and in time the fire burned through the control runs to the tail surfaces, leading to loss of control.

To protect the rear fuselage tanks, a 5 ft (1.5 m) length of 5 mm steel plating was applied externally. Some reports suggest that similar plating was added between the engines, to reduce the chance of damage to one affecting the other.

It has been claimed by the Sukhoi OKB that, although large numbers of Su-25s suffered damage from Stingers, only 22 SAF examples

---

Five weapon stations under each wing give the Su-25 a reasonable load carrying ability up to a maximum of 9700 lb (4400 kg). This example is sequencing its undercarriage and carries two 132 gal (600 lit) drop tanks.

---

were actually lost in the entire course of this nine-year campaign, and that not one was lost after the introduction of the rear fuselage armour.

The claimed loss-rate is stated to represent only one aircraft per 2800 hr of operational flying, indicating that the total operational flying time was 61,600 hr. If there were about 40 Su-25s in Afghanistan, this would suggest an average operational flying rate of 170 hr/yr per aircraft, which sounds reasonable. It may be noted that US Army sources claim that approximately 340 Stingers were fired during this conflict, and that around 269 Soviet and Afghan aircraft were shot down, but the two sets of figures are not necessarily contradictory. Aside from the fact that every apparent hit may have been claimed as a kill, it is likely that most of the losses were helicopters. Furthermore, there were many fixed-wing types serving in Afghanistan, and of

Wearing a different camouflage scheme to the aircraft in the previous picture, this Su-25 is touching down with its wingtip-mounted petal airbrakes extended. The outboard pylon 'shoe' is not fitted, this location being almost exclusively for defensive *Aphid* (AA-8) AAMs.

these the Su-25 was certainly the best protected.

As described in Sukhoi press material, the Su-25 has always had fairly comprehensive protective measures, which represent approximately 7.5 per cent of the normal take-off weight, or 2415 lb (1095 kg). The comparable figure for the A-10 is 2887 lb (1310 kg). The pilot is protected by a welded 24 mm titanium 'bathtub' and a bulletproof windscreen and quarterlights. The bathtub is claimed to withstand 20 mm strikes, and to protect against 30 mm at grazing angles

less than 30 degrees. The rear part of the hood appears to be made of armour plate, hence the pilot is far less exposed than in the case of the A-10, but he has a correspondingly limited rear view.

Vital systems are also protected by armour, the flying controls are actuated via 40 mm diameter titanium rods that are proof against 12.7 mm strikes, and the pitch control rods are duplicated. The Su-25 began life with all-manual controls, but power-assisted ailerons were introduced later, with manual reversion. The fuel tanks are filled with plastic foam to prevent vapour explosions, and there are fire-protection systems (Freon gas) for the engine bays and the spaces around the fuel tanks.

The Su-25 is of conventional design, the only innovation being the use of tip-mounted clamshell-type airbrakes with trailing-edge tabs.

The wing thickness/chord ratio is clearly less than the 16 per cent of the A-10. A twin-barrel 30 mm gun is built into the lower front fuselage, slightly offset to the left, and fed from a magazine containing 250 rounds. It has a cyclic rate of 3000 rd/min, its capacity being reckoned to be sufficient for five attacks, using one-sec bursts. The fixed gun can be supplemented by pylon-mounted 23 mm cannon with 260 rounds per pod. The brochure phrase 'flexible gun mounts' presumably indicates that the cannon can be depressed for strafing.

In addition to two small outboard pylons for self defence AA-2/8 *Atoll/Aphid* missiles, the Su-25 has eight underwing pylons, each stressed for a nominal 1100 lb (500 kg) load. Maximum external load is 9700 lb (4400 kg), but there are proposals to increase this figure to 14,110 lb (6400 kg). Normal external load is currently a modest 3100 lb (1400 kg), but the aircraft can carry eight 1100 lb (500 kg) or 32 × 220 lb (100 kg) bombs, rockets up to 370 mm calibre, or laser-guided air-to-surface missiles weighing 770 or

OPPOSITE AND BOTTOM LEFT Show at Paris in 1989 was a two-seat version of *Frogfoot*, known as the Su-25UT. This was being promoted as an advanced trainer and carried the Bureau designation Su-28. Note the nosewheel mudguard, a standard feature of many Soviet military aircraft. (*Tony Holmes*)

BELOW The 1960s-period panel of the Su-25 showing the large reflector sight in front of the armoured glass windscreen, the short control stick in the centre, engine throttles bottom left and the paired actuating handles for the K-36D ejection seat lower centre. (*Ian Black*)

1435 lb (350 or 650 kg). The aircraft nose houses a laser ranger/designator linked to the GGS. At least four of the pylons appear to be plumbed for droptanks.

The impresion given when the Su-25 made its debut at Le Bourget in 1989 was that the principal weapon is the laser-homing missile, which is possibly a variant of the AS-7 *Kerry* or AS-10 *Karen*. Both types are thought to weigh approximately 900 lb (410 kg), and to deliver a 200 lb (90 kg) warhead over a maximum range of perhaps 5 nm (9 km). Assuming a stabilized laser designator close to the target, average miss distance should be around 16.5 ft (5.0 m). The importance attributed to the laser-homing weapon may support the theory that the role of the Su-25 is to destroy defensive hardpoints (eg, infantry with ATGWs) rather than tanks.

As mentioned earlier, all essential GSE items may be carried in four pylon-mounted pods giving a self-contained dispersal capability that Britain's Harrier might well envy. One pod contains covers for the intakes, cockpit, etc, plus tools and some small spares. Another houses the APU and an electrical generator. The third contains an electrically-driven fuel pump and hoses for refuelling the aircraft from pillow tanks or Red Army tankers. The fourth pod holds the automatic test equipment that has become a feature of Soviet combat aircraft, however simple.

Considerably enhancing the feasibility of front-line dispersal, the engines can be run on diesel fuel or mogas for a limited period, although they may subsequently have to be scrapped.

Normal take-off weight is given as 32,200 lb (14,600 kg), and maximum is 38,800 lb (17,600 kg). Maximum range while carrying the maximum combat load plus two droptanks is 400 nm (750 km) at low level or 675 nm (1250 km) at altitude. Maximum speed at low level is 526 knots (975 km/hr), which is far healthier than the 368 knots (682 km/hr) of the thick-wing turbofan-powered A-10. Maximum load factor is 6.5G with normal load, reducing to 5.2G with maximum load. Service ceiling is given as 23,000 ft (7000 m), perhaps suggesting that the cockpit is unpressurized. The Su-25 can take-off and land with a ground roll of only 2000 ft (600 m), and one report indicates that the use of twin-cruciform parachutes can reduce landing roll to 1500 ft (450 m).

The single-seater (which is flown by both SAF and Naval Aviation), is designated *Frogfoot A*, while *Frogfoot B* refers to the Su-25UB, which is used for weapons training and FAC duties, and is equipped with an arrester hook. The export single-seater, reportedly designated Su-28, has been sold to several countries, including Czechoslovakia, Iraq and North Korea. The two-seater exhibited at Paris in 1989 was the prototype Su-25UT, which had first flown on 6 August 1985, and is apparently being promoted as an advanced trainer to complement the L-39 in Warsaw Pact services. It has the same laser nose shape, but the sensor window is blanked off, and there is no arrester hook.

The single-seater at Le Bourget was said to have been the last production aircraft, yet to have been damaged twice in Afghanistan (once by ground fire and once by an AIM-9 fired by a Pakistani F-16). Assuming that the Sukhoi representative's remarks were translated accurately, this implies that the line closed down in 1988 at the latest. Several hundred Su-25s appear to have been built, but there is no accurate guide to the total, nor is it known whether those built with R-95 engines are being modified to take the R-195. Recent reports indicate that production is, in fact, continuing. The Su-25UT is reportedly being considered as an advanced trainer for both the SAF and the paramilitary flying organisation DOSAAF. In addition, an Su-25 has been used for deck-landing trials on the carrier *Tbilisi*, and these tests could lead to the production of a 'marinized' variant.

To summarize, the Su-25 is a smaller, lighter, and considerably faster equivalent of the A-10, its speed benefiting from a much thinner wing section, higher thrust/weight ratio, and use of turbojet engines (although this clearly penalizes SFC). The Su-25 is noteworthy for its unique ability to operate from dispersed sites with the minimum of support, and for its survivability modifications, which provide a staggering indication of how many flares need to be carried for today's close support role.

ABOVE Quite possibly the best COIN aircraft in the world, this Su-25 *Frogfoot* was evidently photographed just after its arrival at Le Bourget in 1989, with its auxiliary tanks dumped on the grass. The small outboard pylons are believed to be used for self-defence air-air missiles. *(Ian Black)*

BELOW A close-up of the extra flare-dispensers added to the Su-25 as a result of experience in Afghanistan. The aircraft originally had a total of 128 rounds mounted internally, but four 32-round units were added over the jetpipes, doubling its capacity. *(Ian Black)*

LEFT This interesting vertical shot of part of the deck of a *Kiev*-class carrier illustrates the remarkably small spanwise dimension of the folded Yak-38 *Forger A*, which requires (in contrast to a Sea Harrier) little more deck area than the Ka-25 *Hormone* that is sitting with its rotors folded, just ahead of the Yak-38s. Another Ka-25 is at upper right, but the helicopter at upper left is a Ka-27 *Helix*. (UK MoD)

RIGHT A mannequin in standard Soviet Air Forces flying gear, sitting in the K-36 seat. On ejection, the pilot's arms and legs are restrained, and an ejection gun augmented by a rocket of 1390 lb (630 kg) thrust takes the seat clear of the cockpit. From housings visible above the dummy's shoulders, telescopic tubes carrying small droques are extended aft to stabilize the seat. The K-36 is usable from zero-zero conditions up to Mach 3, assuming suitable pilot protective gear. (Tony Holmes)

A thoughtful-looking Anatoly Kvochur (in blue flying overalls) walks towards the business-end of the single-seat MiG-29 *Fulcrum* demonstrator at Le Bourget in 1989. On June 8th Kvochur almost ran out of luck, when the right engine surged as he attempted to accelerate out of a low, slow pass. His life was saved by the remarkable K-36D ejection seat. (Ian Black)

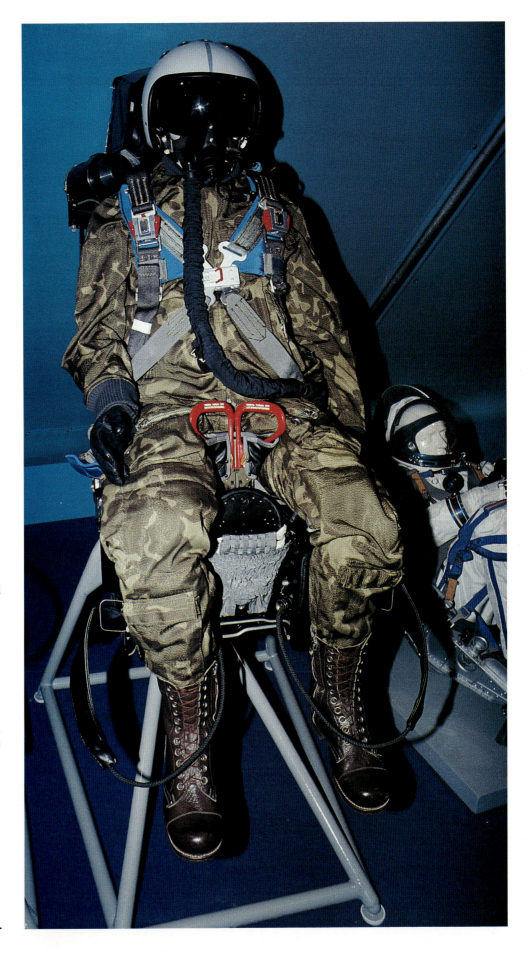

LEFT, MAIN PICTURE **The cockpit enclosures of the two-seat Su-27B, with the combined IRST sensor and laser-ranger mounted just ahead of the conical windscreen. Note the lateral bulging of the windscreen arch to enhance downward view.** *(Tony Holmes)*

LEFT, INSET **Front quarter view of the hump-backed Su-27UB, with the tip-rail of the single-seat Su-27 in the foreground.** *(Ian Black)*

ABOVE **Probably the most noteworthy two-seater extant, the Su-27UB combines a well-drooped front fuselage with a highly elevated rear cockpit, eliminating the need for the mirror system of the MiG-29UB. Note the massive airbrake and the guard on the single nosewheel.** *(Tony Holmes)*

BELOW **The Su-27UB touches down at Farnborough with the traditional puff of burnt rubber, its F-15 Eagle-type airbrake fully extended, and (on this occasion) its afterburner nozzles well clear of the ground.** *(Tony Holmes)*

ABOVE The Su-27UB blasts off the runway in a zero-flap take-off, its mainwheels already beginning to retract. Note the permanent fit of the wingtip launch rails, which reduce the need for torsional stiffness. *(Tony Holmes)*

A sectioned example of the R-33 turbofan, as exhibited at Hanover's ILA-90. The R-33 was developed by the Leningrad bureau, which was historically referred to by its chief engineer's name, originally Klimov, and later Isotov. It is believed that the AL-31F of the Su-27 (which has 50% more thrust) uses a scaled-up version of the low-pressure compressor of the R-33 *(Roy Braybrook)*

5 The New Generation

THE SOVIET types that made their first flights in the period 1975–85 may be regarded as the fourth postwar generation of combat aircraft, and in the case of fighters this represents the third supersonic phase. The basic airframe-engine changes for supersonic capability, such as thin swept wings and afterburners, had been introduced in the 1955–65 period, and shorter field-lengths had been restored in 1965–75. With the new fighters it was a case of developing better radars, giving a long-range look-down, shoot-down multiple-engagement capability, while exploiting new engines of much higher thrust/weight ratio, and making use of fixed, moderately-swept wings. It had taken Soviet designers a long time to discover what Hawker, Dassault and McDonnell Douglas had known for many years, that a moderately swept wing gives an outstanding compromise between the characteristics of un-swept and highly swept planforms, without the weight penalty and complexity of variable-sweep.

The two fighters that exemplify this new generation are the MiG-29 *Fulcrum* and Su-27 *Flanker*, and they are characterized primarily by a quantum leap in agility. They were probably inspired by the examples of the F-14, F-15, F-16 and F/A-18, although these Soviet fighters appear to have achieved better handling characteristics at high AOA than any of their US contemporaries. In a chronological sense, these highly manoeuvrable air superiority fighters were joined by the MiG-31 *Foxhound* air defence fighter, though the latter is vastly different in concept, being a major derivative of the Mach 2.8 MiG-25 *Foxbat*.

During this period the Soviets also flew their first supersonic strategic bomber, the four-engined Tu-160 *Blackjack*, a long-range complement for the smaller, twin-engined *Backfire*. They also began test flights with the Mi-28 *Havoc*, a direct response to America's AH-64 Apache, and thus the Soviet Union's first dedicated attack helicopter.

Foxhound

The first indication that the West had of the existence of a 'Super Foxbat' came from the debriefing of Lt Belyenko, following his flight to Japan in 1976 in his *Foxbat A*. By his account, this derivative aircraft differed in having a stiffened airframe to permit much higher speeds at low level, and more powerful turbojets, giving an afterburning thrust of 30,865 lb (14,000 kg) each. In addition, the radar was said to be much improved, and a ventral arrangement of long-range AAMs was introduced to allow for the carriage of up to six (with two on the wings).

It now appears that the uprated engines and an improved radar were introduced on the MiG-25 production line, resulting in the *Foxbat E* mentioned in Chapter 3, while a more drastic redesign was undertaken to combine a better radius of action, a heavier weapon load, and a longer radar acquisition range, though at some cost in maximum speed. The NATO reporting name *Foxhound* was allocated in 1982, and it was subsequently learned that the official designation is MiG-31.

In essence, the MiG-31 is a considerably lengthened and much heavier two-seat deriva-

Four *Aphid* (AA-8) short-range 'dogfight' missiles underwing and four long-range *Amos* (AA-9) AAMs under the fuselage form the standard armament of the MiG-31. The bulge well aft on the starboard side contains a GSh-623 cannon. The MiG-31s phased-array radar is the first such application in an operational fighter

tive of the MiG-25 single-seater, with provisions for up to four AA-9 *Amos* long-range AAMs under the fuselage. The MiG-31 has four underwing pylons. Each inboard pylon carries an AA-6 *Acrid* medium-range AAM or an auxiliary tank. Each outer pylon can carry two AA-8 *Aphid* short-range AAMs.

The second crew member is inserted aft of the (unchanged) pilot position, and is thus between the intake ducts. In at least some MiG-31s, the back-seater has a retractable periscope. This systems operator was probably added to get the best possible performance out of the radar, which some sources claim is based on stolen Hughes

technology. According to Anatoly Belosvet of the Mikoyan OKB, the system can track 10 targets and engage four simultaneously.

Ground shots of the MiG-31 show twin mainwheels in a peculiar staggered arrangement, with the inboard wheel well forward, to prevent rutting on soft runway surfaces. The basic wing planform appears to be unchanged from the MiG-25, but the flaps and ailerons have been extended spanwise. Small leading edge root extensions have been fitted, perhaps to improve handling at high AOA.

TOP RIGHT The Tu-28P *Fiddler* remains the largest fighter in the world, its size driven by the need for a long radius of action and the weight of its AA-5 *Ash* long-range missiles.

RIGHT Defecting Soviet pilot Viktor Belenko first alerted the West about an advanced two-seat fighter version of the *Foxbat* in 1976. The MiG-31 subsequently appeared and was given the NATO name *Foxhound*.

The 1990 Farnborough Show saw the return of the MiG-29s accompanied by two Su-27s (background). Detail points about the MiG-29UB in the foreground include the cannon blast suppressor air duct in the wing leading edge, the periscope fairing in the rear seat canopy, the triple *Odd-rods* IFF aerial under the nose and the broad UHF aerial just behind. (*Tony Holmes*)

Series production began about 1980 in parallel with the MiG-25 at Gorkiy, 250 miles (400 km) east of Moscow. Deliveries commenced in early 1983. The Air Defence Force is now believed to have around 200 in service, but the MiG-31 has not yet been exported.

The MiG-31 is estimated to be approximately 7 ft (2.15 m) longer than the MiG-25, and has a maximum take-off weight of 101,850 lb (46,200 kg). It has a maximum speed of Mach 2.83 at altitude, and Mach 1.22 at low-level. Intercept radius is 390 nm (720 km) using a Mach 2.35 cruise, or up to 755 nm (1400 km) with two external tanks and a subsonic cruise (Mach 0.85).

When he was US Asst Sec for Defense for C³I, Donald Latham rated the MiG-31 above all US fighters, including the F-15, saying that the Soviet aircraft has 'better avionics, a better C³ system, a better AAM, greater combat range, and they are producing it like gangbusters'. He also said that 'the USSR is now ahead of the USA in the key areas of IR sensors, medium-range AAMs, and the application of digital technology'. However, Latham probably overstated both the MiG-31's capabilities and Soviet technology in some respects.

Fulcrum

In practical aviation terms, *glasnost* became a reality on Tuesday, 30 August 1988, when Aeroflot flights 6241 and 6243 in the form of a MiG-29 *Fulcrum A* and a two-seat MiG-29UB *Fulcrum B* arrived at Farnborough, escorted by two Tornado F.3s of No 5 Sqn. In the following week the Mikoyan pilots staggered the crowds with the MiG-29's tail-slide, something never before demonstrated in the West by a supersonic fighter at low altitude.

Here at last was a Soviet fighter that could compete (at least in terms of airshow demonstrations) with the best that American and European manufacturers could produce. Not only did this aircraft have a thrust/weight ratio higher than even an early model F-16, but it was also fully controllable at far higher attitudes than any Western fighter could utilize. Service AOA

clearance is understood to be 30° less 0.3 times the pitch rate.

Its cockpit was a throwback to the F-4 generation, its radar might not compare with the Hughes APG-65 of the F/A-18, and its missiles were a completely unknown quantity, but the 1988 debut of the MiG-29 ended the general belief in a Western lead in combat aircraft.

According to Sukhoi representatives speaking at Le Bourget in 1989, the basic configuration adopted for the new Soviet air superiority fighters originated at their bureau, but was leaked by TsAGI to the Mikoyan bureau and used in the design of the MiG-29. The configuration featured a moderately swept wing with large LEX, providing attitude-shielding for two widely-separated

'Hey, Leader, have I got news for you!' A 'spot the difference' formation with a tank-equipped *Fulcrum A* forming a vic with two Canadian Forces CF-18A Hornets.

two-dimensional multi-shock intakes, and two vertical tails.

The *Fulcrum A* is essentially a Hornet-size aircraft with far more thrust than the early production F/A-18, and with considerably less fuel. The MiG-29 design places overriding emphasis on the short-range air combat role. The F/A-18's advanced APG-65 radar and AIM-120 missiles clearly make the Hornet a more potent fighter in medium-range intercepts, but it is more evenly balanced between the air-to-surface and air-to-air roles. The Hornet also has a much more advanced cockpit.

The first flight date (as quoted to British writer Jon Lake by CTP Valery Menitsky) was 6 October 1977. The pilot was Pyotr Fedotov, who died in a flying accident in 1984. The first published references to the MiG-29 appeared in 1979, after prototypes had been photographed by US satellites over Ramenskoye.

Before the press briefings at Farnborough, most information on the MiG-29 came from Yugoslav and Polish technical journals. They reported that the aircraft entered service at Kubinka (the SAF show-base outside Moscow) in 1984. Two years later the MiG-29 began its travels, with a six-aircraft visit to Finland, and a 23-aircraft deployment to Wittstock in East Germany.

The MiG-29 is described in the Mikoyan leaflet as a single-seat twin-engined air superiority fighter, with high agility, and such a high thrust/weight ratio that acceleration is possible in a vertical climb. (This is something even an

Debris ingestion prompted the MiG designers to incorporate retractable intake doors which are closed for take-off and landing, air for the Isotov R-33s coming from intake louvres in the top surface of the wing. The location is Abbotsford, Canada.

F-16 cannot do). It has a look-down, shoot-down fire control system. Its coherent pulse-Doppler radar (evidently designated NO-193 or *Slot Back*, and not present in the two-seater) provides a theoretical maximum detection range of 54 nm (100 km) against fighter-size targets. A Yugoslav report states that the radar can track 10 targets simultaneously.

In clear weather use can be made of an IRST, which coupled with laser ranging and a helmet-mounted sight (HMS). The IRST allows the pilot to minimize the use of radar, and the combination of IRST and laser-ranging provides very accurate gunfiring. Deputy chief designer Mikhail Romanovich Waldenberg (believed to be the engineer in charge of the design) stated at Farnborough in 1988 that, if they had known how accurate it would be, they would have halved the size of the magazine.

The MiG-29 can carry up to six AAMs, and has a single 30 mm cannon in the left-hand LEX. It is capable of air-to-ground attacks with bombs, or rockets of 57, 80 and 240 mm calibre.

Since authentic Soviet data on modern combat aircraft is rarely seen, it is perhaps worth recording here. The MiG-29 has a wingspan of 37.27 ft (11.36 m) an overall length of 56.82 ft (17.32 m) including the nose probe, and a height of 15.52 ft (4.73 m). The two-seater is only slightly longer, at 57.14 ft (17.42 m). Wheel track is 10.17 ft (3.10 m).

Normal take-off weight is given as approximately 33,000 lb (15,000 kg), rising to a maximum of around 39,000 lb (18,000 kg). Thrust/weight

ratio is in excess of 1.1:1, and maximum speed is over Mach 2.3. Maximum IAS is more than 800 knots (1500 km/hr), corresponding to Mach 1.22 at sea level. Service ceiling is 56,000 ft (17,000 m). Maximum rate of climb is 65,000 ft/min (330 m/sec). Take-off run is 790 ft (240 m) and landing run is 1970 ft (600 m), presumably using the cruciform parachute, which appears to be

TOP LEFT On both sides of the fuselage adjacent to the MiG-29s cockpit, there are large dynamic pressure probes for the aircraft's flight control system. On the right is the stand-by pitot head.
(*Tony Holmes*)

LEFT Whereas MiG put their cannon in the port wing root, Sukhoi opted for the starboard side with the venting air louvres extending back from the 30 mm muzzle.
(*Tony Holmes*)

Offset to starboard, the IRST (infrared search-and-track) is a primary sensor for clear weather use. Its range is reportedly 15 nm (28 km). On the right-hand side is a temperature probe.
(*Tony Holmes*)

standard practice. Maximum range is about 1130 nm (2100 km).

Further information may be taken from various Yugoslav journals published in May 1988. The MiG-29 wing area was given in the journal *Start* as 409 sq ft (38 m²), presumably without the LEX, which is said to be referred to as a 'sabre'. Yugoslav magazines were probably the first to refer to the engines as 18,300 lb (8300 kg) R-33s, which allow the aircraft to make a vertical climb to 13,000 ft (4000 m). However, they attributed the R-33s to Tumansky, whereas it is now known that the Isotov bureau in Leningrad was responsible. The R-33 is believed to have a dry

This photograph of a navalized MiG-29 on the side lift of the 65,000-ton *Tbilisi* illustrates the aircraft's folding wings and the absence of overwing strakes and auxiliary air inlets. In the background is a Ka-27 *Helix-B* plane-guard/SAR helicopter.

weight of 2326 lb (1055 kg) and a dry thrust of 11,240 lb (5100 kg), associated with an SFC of 0.77 lb/hr/lb. This figure, coupled with the 63 per cent afterburner boost, indicates that the R-33 must be a low bypass turbofan.

At ILA-90 the writer was informed that the R-33 engine was designed by the Leningrad bureau under the leadership of Starovoitenko, but that it is built by the Tschernyschew factory in Moscow. The fuel control system was developed by the Kristall bureau, but is manufactured at the Revolutionbanner plant, also in Moscow. The combined APU/starter is designated GTDE-117, and is located on the aircraft centre-line, providing a shaft-drive to both engines.

Soviet pilots are reported to have zoomed the MiG-29 to 124,640 ft (38,000 m). *Start* gives it an empty weight of 24,000 lb (10,900 kg) and a standard take-off weight of 34,400 lb (15,600 kg). Landing speed is given as 108 knots (200 km/hr), but the figure of 127 knots (235 km/hr) published in Western reports at Farnborough appears more credible.

The MiG-29 and -29UB were ferried to Farnborough '88 with only a centreline tank each, but those flown to ILA-90 (probably direct from Moscow) had a centreline tank that a Mikoyan representative said was of 330 Imp gal (1500 litre) capacity and a pair of underwing 176 Imp gal (800 litre) tanks. The writer was also told that the centre tank is directly in the path of the exhaust from the GTDE-117 starter, so these gases are ducted through the empty rear bay of the tank and expelled from the tail-end. Radius of action is reported as 375 nm (700 km).

Again according to Yugoslav reports, the pilot is warned by IR sensor when an AAM is launched toward his aircraft though this has not been confirmed. He also has an SPO-15 radar-warning receiver, which is now standard on most Soviet fighters, and a voice warning system dubbed 'Natasha'.

Internal fuel capacity is reportedly about

1100 Imp gal (5000 litres), which—if true—is 20 per cent less than that for the F/A-18. Some experts believe its capacity is less. It is also said to be able to carry up to four tanks of 108/176/253 Imp gal (490/800/1150 litres) capacity, but four of the largest size would exceed the aircraft's weight limit. More credible are reports that the cannon magazine holds 150 rounds, and that the aircraft normally carries two medium-range AA-7/10 *Apex/Alamo* missiles in combination with four short-range AA-8/11 *Aphid/Archer* dogfight missiles.

At the time of the *Tbilisi* trials, it was reported that the MiG-29 was being landed at 130 knots (240 km/hr) and an AOA of about 13.5°, compared to a normal speed of 151–156.5 knots (280–290 km/hr) at 11° AOA.

The 'hot' end of an R-33 viewed from the variable-area afterburner nozzle.
(*Roy Braybrook*)

OVERLEAF, LEFT *Fulcrum's* rearward-retracting main undercarriage wheel.

OVERLEAF, RIGHT Double insurance against foreign object ingestion into the engine intakes, despite the doors, is afforded by the mudguard on the MiG-29's steerable nosewheel. The gear retracts aft, pushed by the hydraulic retraction jack on the left.
(*Tony Holmes*)

The most striking aspect of the data published is perhaps the comparison of the MiG-29 and F/A-18 in terms of external loads. The Soviet aircraft takes a modest 6600 lb (300 kg) on seven stations, while F/A-18 takes up to 16,000 lb (7300 kg) on nine. This bears out the emphasis on air superiority in the case of the MiG-29. Comparing the MiG-29 with the much larger Su-27, it is noteworthy that the former cannot take a second (tandem) store on the centreline, has no hardpoints below the intake ducts, and has no wingtip missile launchers.

In some respects this configuration works better for the larger aircraft, in the sense that the gap between the MiG-29's nacelles is too small to permit large stores on the centreline, but rather large from an engine-out handling viewpoint. The asymmetry problem was dramatized by the accident at Le Bourget on 8 June 1989, when Mikoyan test pilot Anatoly Kvochur was making a slow pass at about 97 knots (180 km/hr) and 27° AOA, well below the single-engine safety speed. Kvochur attempted to accelerate for a loop, and the right engine flamed out, due to bird-ingestion damage. His height at this time was about 580 ft (180 m). With full power applied to the left engine to prevent further loss of speed, sideslip came on immediately, and dihedral effect (rolling moment due to sideslip) flipped the aircraft into a dive. Fortunately the aircraft impacted well short of the spectators, and Kvochur's K-39D seat (though delayed by the need to eject the hood) saved his life in a near-horizontal ejection at a height of about 300 ft (90 m).

To digress, the K-36 series of seats (developed by the Zvezda bureau) has been a standard fit on Soviet combat aircraft since about 1980, though it is very heavy by Western standards. The K-36D weighs 450 lb (205 kg). It is armed simply by rotating the crotch handle to the vertical; there are no seat pins. It is ejected by the usual telescopic gun, assisted by a rocket of 1390 lb (630 kg) thrust. Instead of a stabilising drogue, the K-36 has two 7 ft (2.15 m) telescopic tubes mounted high on the seat, which extend aft as soon as it is clear of the aircraft, and deploy small drogues. At high level, the pilot is held in the seat until it descends to 16,400 ft (5000 m), but at low level the pilot is released immediately and the parachute is deployed ballistically, as in the case of the Stencel seat.

The K-36 system is cleared to a maximum height of 82,000 ft (25,000 m) and speed limits of Mach 2.5 and 700 knots (1300 km/hr) IAS when the pilot is wearing a conventional bonedome and oxygen mask, or Mach 3 and 755 knots (1400 km/hr) IAS with a pressurized helmet offering full protection.

One of many interesting design features of the MiG-29 is the closing of the main intakes during take-off and landing, in order to minimize FOD problems and water ingestion. It appears that the intake part of ramp is rotated, so that it closes the inlet completely, when the weight is on the undercarriage and the engine is running at more than idling speed. Air is then supplied to the engines through an array of auxiliary spring-loaded inlets in the upper wing surface, where they are completely free from debris, slush, etc. A considerable effort was dedicated to ensuring a smooth flow from these intakes to the engine. This was so successful that static thrust is claimed to be slightly higher than if the air was taken through the main inlets. However, it seems likely that the average thrust during take-off is somewhat reduced.

When the MiG-29's engines are stopped, the main intakes open automatically to allow visual inspection of the front fan stages. As the engines are accelerated beyond idling speed, the ramps are slammed down, a fast action being necessary to minimize the transient flow distortion at the engine face. The ramps are normally raised at 108 knots (200 km/h), but can be selected closed at speeds up to 430 knots (800 km/h) if a flock of birds is encountered.

It could be said that the Mikoyan team took a long, hard look at all the American Teen-Series fighters before designing the MiG-29. The wing planform with its high taper and moderate sweep is reminiscent of the F-15, though perhaps closer to the F-4 that served as the jumping-off point for the Eagle. The way in which the tail surfaces are carried on outboard booms well aft of the engine nozzles is very much a McDonnell trademark, again derived from F-4 experience. The widely-separated engines of the MiG recall the F-14 configuration, but it is only the F/A-18 that employs the LEX to straighten the air flow into the intakes. The form of the MiG LEX is,

For the markings 'buff', the star is probably authentic on this MiG-29UB, but the number 304 was applied for the 1989 Paris Air Show and was allocated by the organizers. Honeycomb and carbon plastic areas are self-evident on this fin and rudder, while the standard NATO 'lift' symbol is carried by the top rudder hinge. At the bottom is the pivot for the all-flying tailplane, which augments roll control at low AOA. (*Tony Holmes*)

however, closer to the wing-body blending chine of the F-16 than the cambered, sharp-edged LEX of the F/A-18.

The wing of the MiG-29 has leading edge flaps covering most of the span, and relatively small trailing edge flaps and ailerons. Roll control is clearly augmented by differential use of the comparatively large tailplane, an idea that is obviously carried over from the swing-wing MiG-23/27. The two fins, canted outboard like those of the F-14, extend forward over the wing in the form of fences, though these serve no aerodynamic purpose, acting simply as housings for upward-firing chaff/flare dispensers. The rudders have been extended in chord since the Finnish visit. The prototype MiG-29 (now in Monino) has Sukhoi-type underfins.

The 'armpit' mounting of the main undercarriage units is reminiscent of the F-14, and results in an aircraft that sits very low on the ground. This must be a serious restriction on landing speed (which has to be kept high to reduce the frequency of nozzle strikes), but it will facilitate navalization. In comparison, the F/A-18 has its main gears mounted on the bottom of the intake ducts, which results in it being unusually high off the deck for naval operations, and necessitates a far-aft mainwheel position.

The mainwheel track of the MiG-29 is virtually identical to that of the F/A-18, but the wheelbase of the MiG is about 30 per cent shorter. This short wheelbase suggests that the original intention was to place the nosewheels (which retract aft) so far to the rear that they would not throw spray into the intakes, which are positioned longitudinally by the LEX. When this ploy failed, the intake doors and auxiliary inlets were introduced.

The fuselage of the MiG-29 is very nicely designed, even in the case of the two-seater, though the view from the rear cockpit is consequently poor on the approach, hence the retractable periscope. The rear-hemisphere view from the single-seater is better than for most preceding Soviet fighters, but not as good as for current US types. Behind the cockpit the fuselage of *Fulcrum A* tapers away sharply, suggesting it contains little fuel. *Fulcrum C* has a hump-back fuselage, reportedly for extra avionics, not fuel.

The vestigial rear end of the fuselage houses the cruciform parabrake and clamshell-type airbrakes.

The current production MiG-29 has conventional (mechanically-signalled) flying controls, but since 1988 the bureau has been flying an 'intermediate MiG-29' with FBW controls and a modernized cockpit with four CRTs in place of the present steam-gauges. It is reported that the tailplane, wing position and CG location have all been changed, presumably to reduce longitudinal stability. References have also been made to a 9G centreline tank, increased take-off weight, and far more extensive use of composite materials than the current 7 per cent.

One known variant is the naval MiG-29 with a folding wing, arrester hook, and probably a stronger undercarriage and special anti-corrosion measures. This aircraft also has bulged wingtips (possibly housing ESM equipment), and the wing strakes are deleted. The overwing auxiliary inlets appear to be deleted, hence the main intakes presumably remain open at all times. A buddy-buddy refuelling system is being developed.

On 21 November 1989, piloted by Toktar Aubakirov, Mikoyan's deputy chief test pilot, this navalized MiG-29 began trials on the new Soviet 'aircraft-carrying cruiser' *Tbilisi*. It subsequently took off unassisted, using the vessel's skijump deck to launch below its normal minimum flight speed. Deck trials were also performed by an Su-27 and Su-25. India is said to be considering the use of MiG-29s on its forthcoming indigenously-designed carrier.

Reports suggest that around 500 MiG-29s have been built for the home market, and that the type has already been exported to Afghanistan, Cuba, Czechoslovakia, East Germany, Hungary, India, Iraq, North Korea, Poland, Romania, Syria and Yugoslavia. However, at time of writing deliveries to Afghanistan are not confirmed, and Hungary is offering some of its MiG-29s for sale. At least one two-seater has been photographed in Czech markings, but in early 1990 the country's defence minister (Miroslav Vacek) declared in Moscow that Czechoslovakia had cancelled its plans to buy the MiG-29. The export price for the single-seater is believed to be approximately $23 million, and for the two-seater $28 million.

Despite the thaw in East-West relations, there is no hard evidence that a MiG-29 has been obtained for technical evaluation before German unification. In this context an interesting opportunity was missed on 20 May 1989, when a Soviet pilot defected with his *Fulcrum A variant 5* from Batum in South Georgia to Trabzon on the Turkish Black Sea coast. Unfortunately for Western experts, SAF representatives were allowed to recover the aircraft immediately. A press report in August 1990 quoted a KGB publication as stating that some MiG-29s had illegally been sold to a foreign agency, but no details were given.

Flanker

The public debut of the Sukhoi Su-27 *Flanker* at the Paris Airshow of June 1989 caused an even greater sensation than the MiG-29 had done at Farnborough in the previous year. Demonstrated by Victor Pugachev (CTP) and Eugeny Frolov, this massive air supremacy fighter was flown

(AOA- and pitch-rate-limiters off) to incredible AOA values at low level and obviously with total confidence. (Service AOA clearance is a more conventional 26°).

The Su-27 was widely judged the finest demonstration aircraft ever, and many observers came away from Le Bourget wondering if it might not also be the world's finest fighter.

The flying of the Su-27 was particularly noteworthy in terms of controllability at low speeds, and the pilot's faith in the stability of their aircraft at extreme nose-high attitudes. Equally significant, they were clearly confident that the engines would continue to function throughout some unprecedented manoeuvres.

Pugachev's 'Cobra' is a dynamic deceleration,

A useful comparison view of the two versions of the Su-27, *Flanker B* in the foreground and *Flanker C* behind. The latter has full combat capability and the raised rear seat gives a good view ahead.
(*Tony Holmes*)

in which the nose of the Su-27 is snatched up from a low level pass at around 240 knots (450 km/hr). With engines idling, the speed falls to around 60 knots (110 km/hr) within three seconds. While this is happening, the aircraft gains some height, but then it mushes forwards in roughly level flight at an altitude of about 120° to the horizontal, moving tail first. Recovery is effected in a very positive nose-down pitch.

On reflection, the explanation for the aircraft's recovery is presumably that the wing AC moves aft from around 25 to 50 per cent chord as AOA increases to 90°, and that this change to positive longitudinal stability is accentuated by the channel-section rear fuselage and elliptic front fuselage. Once it reaches really high AOA values, the Su-27 thus desperately wants to get its nose down, and whether the tailplane helps at all is debatable.

However, this is not to say that pitch control is not highly effective at more normal AOA values. This was very evident in the Su-27's slow-speed flypasts at Le Bourget, which were initially performed at a remarkable 80 knots (150 km/hr), though they were later increased to 97 knots (180 km/hr) after Kvochur's accident in the MiG-29. Tailplane travel for the Su-27 is reported to be plus 16° and minus 21°.

On the subject of handling characteristics, we now have the word of the RAAF CAS (Air Marshal Ray Funnell), who flew the Su-27UB briefly at Singapore in early 1990, that 'the Su-27 is a delightful aircraft to fly'.

Just as impressive as the aircraft itself is Sukhoi's chief designer, Mikhail Petrovich Simonov, who was born on 19 October 1929 and joined the bureau in 1970. At Le Bourget he was perfectly willing to admit to the Su-27's current deficiencies in terms of cockpit instrumentation (and consequently high workload), but was very evidently proud of his bureau's product, and of the fact that his organization had succeeded in attaining equality with the best of Western manufacturers.

The Su-27 is the Soviet Union's equivalent of the F-15, but somewhat larger, and with a better performance in some areas. Its history goes back to 1969, when preliminary design work was carried out under the direction of Pavel Osi-

povich Sukhoi, whose name the bureau still carries. To put this timescale into perspective, the F-14 first flew on 21 December 1970, and the F-15 on 27 July 1972, though information on these aircraft was publicly available long before they flew.

Configurational thinking at the Sukhoi OKB must have been influenced not only by these aircraft, but also by the F-16 and Northrop YF-17, which had their maiden flights on 2 February 1974 and 9 June 1974 respectively. These smaller aircraft introduced the concept of large leading edge extensions on moderately swept wings.

However, an equally important element of the new Sukhoi design was the use of FBW controls, which in the US fighter context were introduced with the YF-16. In essence, FBW makes possible a longitudinally unstable aircraft, which not only responds faster, but flies with an upload on the tailplane, thus achieving more lift and less trim drag. In principle, negative stability could also be applied in a directional sense, allowing a possibly smaller vertical tail. This was considered for the EFA (the mockup was shown at one stage with a small all-moving fin), but the idea appears to have been rejected.

The Sukhoi bureau's experience with FBW goes back many years, to the Su-100, a canard/slender delta technology demonstrator for a Mach 3 interceptor to compete with the more conventional MiG-25, or possibly to offer an advanced replacement for that aircraft. In any event, the Su-100 eventuated much later, making its first flight on 22 August 1972. Flight trials continued for several years, and a speed of Mach 3.3 was reached, but then the two prototypes were placed in storage. A photograph of the Su-100 was included in an exhibition of Sukhoi designs in Moscow in 1982, and more recently one of the prototypes has been placed in the Monino Museum.

Rear cockpit of the Su-27UB *Flanker C*. Internal layout is rather dated compared with western equivalents, but it probably works well for the average Soviet Air Force pilot. The control stick appears almost identical to that in the Su-25 *Frogfoot*. (*Ian Black*)

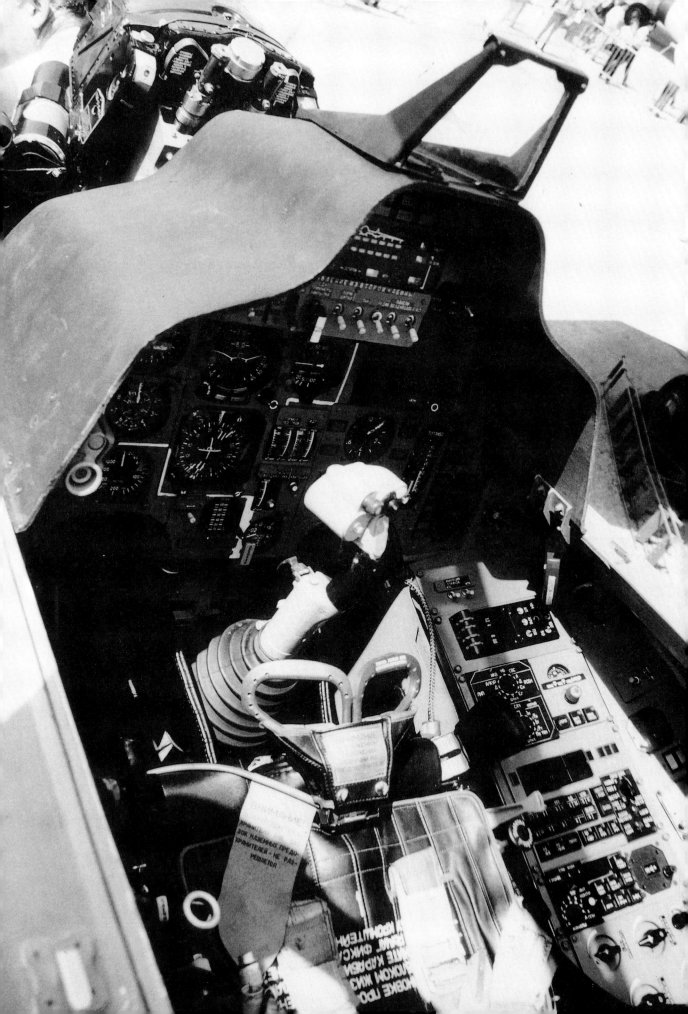

The Su-27 reportedly began life as the private-venture Type 1021, though it firmed up under the OKB designation T-10. The design approach was to optimize the wing planform, then add a well-blended fuselage and LEX, and intakes that would permit operation at high AOA. Considerable emphasis was placed on having sufficient internal fuel to provide excellent range and endurance without recourse to droptanks. The distance between the engine nacelles was dictated by the need to achieve acceptable drag while carrying two centreline AAMs in tandem.

The aircraft was designed from the outset to have negative longitudinal stability, exploiting the bureau's FBW experience. The flight controls were to be based on triplex analogue FBW in roll and yaw, with mechanical connections providing backup, and quadruplex FBW in pitch. In the case of a longitudinally unstable aircraft there is, of course, no point in providing mechanical signalling in pitch, since the pilot cannot react quickly enough to stabilize the aircraft. In the case of the British Aerospace EAP it was estimated that, without synthetic stability, the load factor on the aircraft would double every half-second.

It has been reported that all prototypes of the Su-27 were refered to by the OKB as T-10s, although the later ones incorporated extensive redesign. The first prototype T-10-1 (*Flanker A*) had its maiden flight on 20 May 1977. As in the case of the Su-25, the pilot was Vladimir Ilyushin. Two of the first three prototypes crashed, but that first aircraft (coded '10') is now on show at Monino, and differs from production Su-25s in several respects.

The vertical tails were initially closer together, mounted on top of the nacelles. The nose undercarriage was mounted immediately behind the radome and retracted aft. The wings had rounded tips, but no leading edge flaps. The doors that

Unlike the two-seat MiG-29UB, the two-seat Su-27 has a complete air intercept system with a radar in the nose and IRST ahead of the windscreen. The nosewheel retracts forward and incorporates the usual mudguard. The Su-27UB's ground crew watch as a BAe Hawk 200 and Harrier GR.5 taxi past during the 1989 Paris Air Show. (*Tony Holmes*)

covered the forward-retracting mainwheels also appear to have functioned as airbrakes. The Monino aircraft (which presumably is in its final flight state) has a single large fence on either wing, though a TV film of an early flight test (in which the aircraft is also coded '10') shows two fences on each side.

Later prototypes were extensively redesigned. Sukhoi representatives have claimed that only the nosewheel and ejection seat remained unchanged. As recounted to this writer by deputy chief designer Constantin C Marbashev at Le Bourget in 1989, the original Su-27 configuration was found to have unsatisfactory directional stability above Mach 2. In consequence the vertical tails were moved from the nacelles to outrigger booms (like those of the MiG-29), though they were not inclined outboard. It may

by noted that the F-15 is probably the only comparable aircraft with truly vertical fins.

To further improve directional stability, underfins were added to these booms, though they restrict rotation at unstick and touchdown to 17°. Unique in this class, a long tail 'sting' was added on the centreline, projecting well aft of the nozzles. It reduces drag and adds useful volume for extra fuel, a braking parachute, and chaff/flare dispensers. The twin underwing airbrakes were replaced by a single dorsal unit, similar to that of the F-15. The nose undercarriage was moved much further aft, to retract forwards. This change may have been necessary because the original location reduced directional stability, or because the nosewheel threw water and debris into the intakes.

For the production aircraft (*Flanker B*) the wingtips were squared off and equipped with AAM launch rails. These appear to be a permanent fit, serving (as in the case of the F-5) as anti-flutter weights. Leading edge flaps were introduced, and wing camber was made automatically variable for optimum turn performance. The engines were also considerably modified, Sukhoi accepting a significant weight penalty to ensure reliability.

The extent of the modifications was such that

A 'mix' of four different types of *Alamo* (AA-10) AAM can arm *Fulcrum* and *Flanker*. The lower example in this view is a radar-guided *Alamo C* while on the inboard pylon is the latest *Alamo D* long-range IR homing round. Two *Archer* short-range IR AAMs can be seen at the top of the picture; *Archer* is understood to be a replacement for *Aphid* (AA-8).

Sukhoi, like MiG, has introduced a FOD-ingestion door within the intake of the Su-27. At lower right is the port-side ECM antenna.
(*Roy Braybrook*)

the production-standard Su-27 made its first flight only on 20 April 1981, four years after the first prototype. Further substantial delays then occurred, due primarily to problems with its very advanced radar, but the Su-27 is said to have entered service in 1984. For comparison, the F-14 entered service at the end of 1972, and the F-15 in 1975.

In view of the often-expressed opinion that the Su-27 is 'only a big MiG-29', it is perhaps worth listing the other differences between them. The fuselages differ in that the Su-27 has a marked nose-droop and hump-backed centre fuselage, and a tail-sting. In the case of the two-seater, the rear crew member of the Su-27UB is raised much higher than in the MiG-29UB, hence the former does not require a periscope.

The wings differ in that the Su-27 has a somewhat higher aspect ratio and rails on squared-off tips, while the MiG has rounded tips and no rails. As noted above, the Su-27 has really vertical tails and underfins, while the tails of the MiG are canted outboard. The single nosewheel of the Su-27 is mounted much further forward and retracts forward, whereas the twin nose-wheels of the MiG provide only a short wheel-base and retract aft. The Su-27 has a single dorsal airbrake, and the MiG has a twin-brake clamshell between the nozzles. The Su-27 has FBW controls, while the current MiG-29 has traditional mechanical signalling.

Turning to armament, the Su-27 has its 30 mm gun on the right with 200 rounds, the MiG the same GS-301 on the left with 150 rounds. The Su-27 can carry two large AAMs in tandem on the centreline and two under the intake ducts (aside from the wingtips and four underwing pylons for smaller weapons), whereas the MiG is limited to a fuel tank on the centreline and relatively small missiles on six underwing pylons.

As in the case of the MiG, it may be worth

reproducing the design bureau's data-summary for the Su-27. The aircraft is described as a fighter-interceptor (though Western reports also refer to it as an escort fighter for the Su-24 *Fencer*). It is officially characterized as having a high thrust/weight ratio, FBW controls with automatic limits on AOA and load factor, automatically-variable wing camber, large-scale use of titanium, 'optical electronic radar', and a helmet-mounted target designator. As in the case of the MiG-29 (and F-16), the Su-27 is designed for operation at up to 9G. The two-seat Su-27UB *Flanker C* retains all the combat capabilities of the single-seater (unlike the MiG case).

Between 1986 and '88, a version designated P-42 established 27 world records for time-to-height and sustained altitude, including five absolute records. Aside from Pugachev and Frolov, the pilots were Oleg Tsoi and Nikolai Sadovnikov. The P-42 was powered by R-32 engines (almost certainly uprated for these flights), and took off at a weight of only 31,110 lb (15,100 kg). The records included the following times-to-height from wheels rolling, and are presented here in comparison with the F-15 'Streak Eagle' record figures from 1975.

Altitude		P-42	F-15
9840 ft	(3000 m)	25.373 sec	27.57 sec
19,680 ft	(6000 m)	30.05 sec	39.33 sec
29,520 ft	(9000 m)	44.176 sec	48.86 sec
39,360 ft	(12,000 m)	55.542 sec	59.38 sec
49,200 ft	(15,000 m)	70.329 sec	77.04 sec

Returning to the Sukhoi handout, the Su-27 has a length without nose-probe of 71.95 ft (21.935 m), a span of 48.2 ft (14.700 m) including missile rails, and a height of 19.46 ft (5.932 m). The two-seater is no longer than the single-seater, but it is slightly taller at 20.85 ft (6.357 m). The Su-27 is thus somewhat larger than the F-15, which is 63.75 ft (19.436 m) long, 42.81 ft (13.053 m) in span, and 18.46 ft (5.628 m) high.

The Su-27 is stated to have a normal take-off weight of 48,500 lb (22,000 kg), where as an F-15C with full internal fuel and four AIM-7s weighs 44,630 lb (20,250 kg). If the larger size of the Su-27 results in a higher empty weight than the 28,600 lb (12,970 kg) of the F-15C, then the take-off figure appears to imply that 'normal' take-off for the Su-27 is associated with considerably less fuel than the full 19,000 lb (8620 kg) reported in the technical press. For comparison, the F-15C without conformal tanks houses about 13,600 lb (6175 kg) of fuel.

The suspicion of partial fuelling is supported by the fact that the two Lyulka (Perm bureau) AL-31F turbofans each provides a thrust of 27,600 lb (12,500 kg), giving the Su-27 a 'normal' thrust/weight ratio of 1.14, compared to 1.065 for the F-15C. The AL-31F was shown in part-sectioned form at an exhibition in Moscow in early 1990. A dry weight of 3375 lb (1530 kg) was given, corresponding to a thrust/weight ratio of 8.17:1, which is no better than for comparable Western engines. The engine was noted to have four fan stages and nine high pressure stages, driven by single-stage turbines.

Maximum take-off weight is given as 66,150 lb (30,000 kg), which might be compared to 68,000 lb (30,840 kg) for the F-15C. The increase of 17,650 lb (8000 kg) relative to 'normal' take-off weight again suggests that the latter is only partially fuelled, since an air combat fighter with a large internal fuel volume is hardly likely to carry such a load externally.

The Su-27 has a maximum speed of Mach 2.35 and a service ceiling of 59,000 ft (18,000 m), whereas the F-15C can touch Mach 2.50 and has a service ceiling of 60,000 ft (18,300 m). Maximum range for the Su-27 is 2160 nm (4000 km), while that given for the F-15C with underwing tanks (not conformal tanks) is 2500 nm (4630 km). However, without knowing the assumptions on reserves, detailed comparisons are impossible.

The production aircraft currently has no flight refuelling provisions, but it can fly over five hours on internal fuel alone, which suggests that the maximum range is computed on that basis. Trials have been carried out with a retractable

The forward-retracting nose undercarriage leg of the Su-27 with tow-bar attached. On the right is the hydraulic retraction jack, at the top of the leg are the twin landing lamps with the single taxiing lamp below.
(*Tony Holmes*)

probe on the left side of the front fuselage, including one flight of 16 hours. This presumably was the demonstration in which the Su-27 flew from Moscow to the east coast and back, a total distance of around 7500 nm (14,000 km). The type of tanker was not published, but there have been references to a buddy pack on the Su-24.

It was stated at Paris '89 that the Su-27 is cleared for day/night operation down to 200 ft (60 m) cloudbase and 900 yd (800 m) visibility. Like the MiG-29, the Su-27 was designed to be able to use badly-surfaced or damaged runways,

RIGHT Touchdown speed for the Su-27UB is around 125 knots (220 km/hr) and landing roll with maximum braking is 1650 ft (500 m).
(*Tony Holmes*)

BELOW The purposeful 'sit' of the Su-27 is emphasized in this view as the two AI-31F turbofans power it down the runway.
(*Tony Holmes*)

though it uses a completely different system for intake protection. Instead of closing the intakes and relying on the flow from auxiliary inlets, the Su-27 has titanium grills to prevent stones that are sucked off the runway entering the engines. These grills normally lie flat in the lower surfaces of the ducts, and are mounted on trunnions at their aft ends. When the engines are started, the grills are raised hydraulically to a position obliquely across the ducts. Any debris is then stopped by the grills and deflected downwards through auxiliary inlets in the bottom of the ducts. After lift-off, microswitches on the main legs retract the grills, and when the undercarriage is selected down for landing the grills are raised again.

The grills produce a thrust-loss of approximately 440 lb (200 kg) per engine, which is felt to be a small penalty for the protection they provide. On the other hand, they do not give the absolute protection of the MiG system, which is effective against the smallest of stones and against water thrown up by the nosewheels. The Sukhoi view appears to be that the sheet-metal

ABOVE To help reduce weight, honeycomb/carbon fibre is used extensively on the Su-27, particularly for the fin and rudder. The light-coloured fin tip contains the VHF aerial.
(*Tony Holmes*)

LEFT Apart from the distinctive nose-droop appearance of the Su-27 compared with the MiG-29, the former can be readily identified by a tail cone extending well behind the engine exhausts.
(*Tony Holmes*)

guard on the nosewheel keeps most of the water clear of the intakes, and that the thrust-loss associated with total intake closure is unacceptable.

The Su-27 handout material also refers to the intakes having a 'blowaway jet system', implying something similar to the Douglas installation developed many years ago for the DC-8. However, the blowaway system was not mentioned at the briefings, and there was no obvious jet nozzle in the lower lip of the intake.

Another interesting feature of the Su-27 is the lateral control system. This is based on single-piece flaperons (no dedicated ailerons), augmented by differential tailplane movement, use of the rudders and (subsonically) by differential use of the leading edge flaps.

The undercarriage is designed for a relatively high descent rate, namely 19.7 ft/sec (6 m/sec), which may imply that the bureau had a naval derivative in mind from the outset. As in the case of the MiG-29, the Su-27 cannot make full use of its minimum flight speed capability when landing, since it is attitude-limited by the ventral fins and afterburner nozzles. On at least one occasion at Le Bourget in 1989 the Su-27 struck the runway with its rear end on touching down, creating a shower of sparks, though evidently without causing significant damage.

Fuel is mainly carried in the centre fuselage and inboard wing panels, supplemented by smaller tanks between the engines. One of the changes made during development was to reposition the accessories (ie, fuel pumps, generators, hydraulic pumps, etc) from below the engine to the top, since this would put them inside the wing and thus reduce frontal area and wave drag. This change also reduced wing fuel, but that was compensated by the introduction of the tailstring, which contains additional fuel. All tanks are filled with polyurethane foam, and there are further protective measures (Freon gas?) in the voids around the tanks.

No details have been revealed concerning the operational equipment of the Su-27. However, the performance of its pulse-Doppler radar clearly benefits from a very large antenna, said to be the largest of any current Soviet fighter except for the MiG-31 *Foxhound*. Most reporters at the

Paris-89 briefing understood that the present weapon system cannot engage two targets simultaneously, though it can switch between targets very quickly. The radar is linked to the pilot's HMS and to the IRST and laser-ranger, which is somewhat larger than that of the MiG-29.

The current cockpit is pure 'steam gauge' in terms of instrumentation, though a modern EFIS-type system was promised for Paris-91. In the two-seat Su-27UB, the rear seat is raised 27.5 inches (70 cm) above the front one, eliminating the need for a periscope. The ejection seats are K-36DM series II.

External weapons can be carried on 10 stations, including two in tandem between the nacelles and two below the intake ducts. Each wing has two pylons and a tip rail. The handout refers to the carriage of up to 10 missiles, including the AA-10 *Alamo* of 'increased range with semi-active radar guidance', the AA-9 *Amos* of 'medium range with semi-active (radar) or passive IR guidance', and the AA-8 *Aphid* 'of short range with passive IR guidance'. Reference was made at the briefing to the AA-11 *Archer* as a possible additional store type, and this missile was later shown on the Su-27 at Frunze.

The Paris briefing including a video showing land-based skijump trials and arrested landings, to test the suitability of the Su-27 for the new carrier *Tbilisi*, which was launched in 1985 and began sea trials in late 1989. One aircraft is known to have been destroyed in an accident during these airfield tests.

Another video showed a modified aircraft, designated T-10-24 and equipped with a variable-incidence foreplane. This aircraft, which first flew in 1986, was shown carrying out take-off and landing tests. Simonov indicated that another trials programme had been carried out using thrust-vectoring, though he implied that the results had not been very impressive.

Pilot and ground crew discuss any last minute problems before the Su-27 gives another admired air show performance.
(*Tony Holmes*)

The means of vectoring were later specified as two-dimensional nozzles, as employed on the F-15S/MTD. Deck trials on the *Tbilisi* began in late 1989, and appear to have involved both a folding-wing Su-27 and the T-10-24. At the end of 1990 it was reported that the foreplane-equipped Su-27 had entered service with Naval Aviation.

Maj-Gen Vladimir Ilyushin, who seems to have made the unlikely transition from CTP to deputy designer-in-chief, has indicated that (thanks to the skijump) the take-off run is only 330–600 ft (100–180 m), depending on weight. This short run benefits from the use of deck-launch 're-strainers', which appear to be hinged planks,

Carrier trials with both the MiG-29 and Su-27 began on the *Tbilisi* in late-1989. The Soviet Union has pioneered the use of a ski-jump to allow high-performance combat aircraft to take-off from a carrier without the operational restrictions of a catapult, although arrestor wires are still required for landing.

raised ahead of the mainwheels to allow the engines to be run up to full thrust before the aircraft is released. Deck-end speed is 75–85 knots (220–240 km/hr).

Other Sukhoi representatives stated that the foreplane had made possible a reduction in approach speed to 130 knots (240 km/hr), though this canard further reduces stability. This comment may well indicate that the T-10-24 is more unstable than desirable at combat speeds, and that it would have to be modified to restore the current production level of instability if it were to be developed for service use.

Again according to Ilyushin, the bureau is considering the development of a centreline buddy refuelling store for use on the navalized Su-27UB. The bureau is known to be developing a variant with side-by-side seating to facilitate carrier training.

Reports have suggested that 'over 100' Su-27s were in service with the Air Defence Force by early 1989, replacing aircraft such as the

As illustrated in this landing shot, carrier trials have been carried out with an Su-27 with foreplanes added. In addition to folding wings, arrestor hook, and strengthened undercarriage, reports indicate that the production naval aircraft may have a limited degree of thrust-vectoring and a flight refuelling capability.

Yak-28P, Su-15 and Tu-28P/128, and performing practice intercepts in conjunction with the Il-76 *Mainstay* AEW aircraft. However, even if Soviet fighter production really has been reduced to around 600 per year, the Su-27 in-service total must be increasing rapidly, as this is surely the principal type being manufactured today.

Sukhoi claims that the Su-27 is only 10 per cent more expensive than the MiG-29 are unbelievable, since the former aircraft is about 50 per cent

heavier. However, the point is probably academic, since (despite the frequency with which it is appearing at international airshows) it is unlikely that the Soviet Union would really export its latest and finest combat aircraft.

In the foregoing discussion the Su-27 has been compared with the F-15 in terms of size, weight, performance, etc, but no overall comparison of the two types in design terms has been attempted. In this context it should perhaps be emphasized that the most important consideration is how the two compare in a medium-range engagement, since (assuming suitable rules of engagement) there is little point in excelling at short-range dogfights if the aircraft does not survive long enough to close with the enemy.

Given equal radars, the F-15 probably has the edge in a BVR firing, since its radar signature benefits from the semi-recessed carriage of AIM-120s in tandem pairs, and since it can engage several targets simultaneously. However, the F-15's advantage is not as significant as it might be, since most F-15s carry pylon-mounted tanks, and the radar cross section of the Su-27 benefits to some extent from the tandem-carriage of two medium-range weapons on the centre-line. These same factors clearly reduce the F-15's possible superiority in regard to drag and acceleration.

In a visual dogfight with short-range missiles and guns, the only advantage of the F-15 appears to be its better cockpit, although this might be leapfrogged by the new-generation cockpit of the Su-27. The Sukhoi aircraft already has the advantage in regard to thrust/weight ratio, FBW controls, better AOA tolerance, a helmet-mounted sight for off-boresight missile designation, laser ranging, and a modern cannon. This multi-faceted superiority is a matter for some concern, since (pending the arrival of the ATF) the F-15 is the best fighter that the West has got.

Blackjack

Technologically the most important bomber in Soviet service is now the Tu-160 *Blackjack*, a four-engined variable-sweep strategic penetrator with a supersonic performance far in excess of its US equivalent, the Rockwell B-1B.

Ironically, the Tu-160 was clearly inspired by the original B-1A, which first flew on 23 December 1974, but was cancelled by President Carter in June 1977. When that programme was resurrected by President Reagan in October 1981, it was on a much less ambitious basis, with maximum speed reduced to Mach 1.25, and the emphasis switched to low level penetration and further reductions in radar cross-section area.

Painted in dark camouflage, Strategic Air Command has a fleet of 95 B-1Bs, deliveries being completed in April 1988. They each have a crew of four and their role is low-level strike.

In the Tu-160 *Blackjack*, Tupolev has produced a design that bears more than a passing resemblance to the American Rockwell B-1B. This Tu-160, like others seen to date, is finished in a very light grey colour, indicating its high-level penetration role.

The emasculated (if stealthy) B-1B first flew on 18 October 1984, and deliveries began in mid-1985.

The Tu-160 (a designation confirmed by Gen-Col P Deynekin, commander of Strategic Aviation), was originally known in the West as Ram-P. A grainy photograph was published in a US journal in late 1981, showing this aircraft on the ground. It was standing close to two Tu-144 supersonic transports, hence the photograph provided a good indication of the aircraft's size.

Fairly accurate artists' impressions of the Tu-160 appeared in *Soviet Military Power* from the 1987 issue, indicating that much better photographs had been acquired by the US. On 2 August 1988 the US Defense Secretary Frank

Carlucci and his USAF aide Maj-Gen Gordon E Fornell were shown over a Tu-160 at Kubinka airbase, 40 miles (65 km) west of Moscow, and two further examples flew overhead. They were told that the aircraft had 'recently' become operational, confirming US intelligence predictions.

The Tu-160 made its public debut in August 1989, when one example took part in the Aviation Day flypast at Tushino. It was disclosed that the aircraft has a maximum weight of 275 tonnes (606,000 lb), a maximum speed of 2200 km/hr (Mach 2.07), and a crew of four.

Very little additional information has been published in the Soviet press, beyond the fact that its role is to penetrate at both high and low levels, and that the engineer in charge of the design was V Bliznyuk. There are also indications that the crew find the seats somewhat uncomfortable on long flights, and that the ground crews are plagued with teething troubles, which the Tupolev team has been slow to sort out.

The Tu-160 is generally similar to the B-1 in configuration, with twin-engine nacelles mounted below the wing, just inboard of the hinges, and the tailplane mounted one-third the way up the fin. Since the main undercarriage units are mounted immediately inboard of the engines, the track is very narrow, possibly placing restrictions on crosswind operations. As in the case of the Tu-22M *Backfire*, each main leg carries six wheels on three axles, retracting into the fuselage. One unusual feature is that yaw control for the Tu-160 is provided by the upper fin, moving as a single slab.

The Tu-160 follows earlier Soviet swing-wing philosophy, in having the hinges well outboard and a very large area of fixed wing. All weapons appear to be carried in two large bays, each of which can house a rotary launcher. In the case of the aircraft shown to Carlucci, the forward bay contained a rotary launcher carrying six AS-15 *Kent* ALCMs. It is understood that the launcher can alternatively take 12 SRAM-type defence-penetration missiles. The launcher occupied only two-thirds of the length of the bay, leaving space for bombs. The subsonic AS-15 has a range in the order of 1600 nm (3000 km), and it may be replaced by the supersonic AS-19. It has been estimated that the Tu-160 can accommodate a warload of approximately 36,000 lb (16,500 kg).

The crew of four sit in standard ejection seats, and gain access to the cabin by means of a hatch in the top of the nosewheel bay, and a walkway running forward between the avionics bays. The cockpit is somewhat more spacious than that of the B-1B, and the aircraft is reportedly flown by means of a fighter-type control column, rather than conventional yokes. Strangely, each pilot has four throttles on his left, rather than using a combined central group.

The other two crew members are thought to be responsible for the defensive and offensive avionics systems. The device under the nose, originally thought to be a visual bomb-aimer's position, was reported to be an EO/FLIR sensor. Carlucci was told that the aircraft had no flight-refuelling provisions, but US intelligence sources refer to a retractable probe in the upper nose, between the radome and the windscreen.

Relating the Tu-160 to the B-1B, the Soviet aircraft is somewhat larger, with a length of approximately 177 ft (54 m) and a maximum span of 182 ft (55.5 m), compared to 147 ft (44.8 m) and 136.7 ft (41.7 m) respectively for the US aircraft. The Tu-160's maximum weight of 606,000 lb (275,000 kg) is 27 per cent heavier than the 477,000 lb (216,300 kg) of the B-1B. The Mach 2.07 capability of the Tu-160 clearly gives it a high level penetration that the Mach 1.25 B-1B lacks, and this role difference is reflected in their different camouflage schemes, the Tu-160 (like the B-1A) being painted white, and the B-1B European One (ie, Dark Olive Green, Dark Green and Dark Grey). The 3950 nm (7300 km) radius estimated for the Tu-160 is approximately 20 per cent greater than the 2500 nm (6000 km) of the B-1B.

The Tu-160 is manufactured at Kazan, some 500 miles (800 km) east of Moscow. The production rate is believed to be much less than 30 per year, which was the peak for *Backfire*. Reports have suggested that 'at least 11' were flying at the time of the Carlucci visit, but this idea may have been based simply on the number '11' having been stencilled on the crew hatch of the aircraft inspected. One Tu-160 is said by US intelligence to have crashed in May 1987.

In late 1989 a Tu-160 made a series of record-breaking flights under the designation *Samalyot* (Aeroplane) 70-03, which possibly indicates that the Tupolev bureau refers to it as the Type 70, and that the third prototype was used. The engines were referred to by the designation P, and the nominal thrust was given as 55,115 lb (25,00 kg), which is 80 per cent above that for the B-1B's F101.

The first flight occurred on 31 October 1989 at Podmoskovnoye, and the pilot was L V Kozlov. Take-off weight was given as 529,100 lb (240,000 kg). The flight included a speed of 934.3 knots (1,731.4 km/hr) — about Mach 1.63 — around a 1000 km closed circuit while carrying a 55,115 lb (25,000 kg) load. For aircraft in the 200–250 metric tons class, further claims related to a horizontal flight altitude of 39,863 ft (21,150 m), the carriage of a load of 67,176 lb (30,471 kg) to 6560 ft (2000 m), and the attainment of a height of 45,583 ft (13,894 m) with a load of 66,138 lb (30,000 kg).

A second flight took place on 3 November 1989, also from Podmoskovnoye, but with B I Veremey as pilot. Take-off weight was 606,000 lb (275,000 kg). The first claim related to a speed of 905.4 knots (1678 km/hr) — about Mach 1.58 — around a 2000 km closed circuit while carrying a 55,115 lb (25,000 kg) load. For the 250–300 kg weight category, further claims related to a horizontal flight altitude of 36,910 ft (11,250 m), the carriage load of 67,176 lb (30,471 kg) to 6560 ft (2000 m), and a height of 45,931 ft (11,000 m) with a load of 66,138 lb (30,000 kg).

Three-view of the Tupolev Tu-160 *Blackjack*. (*Pilot Press*)

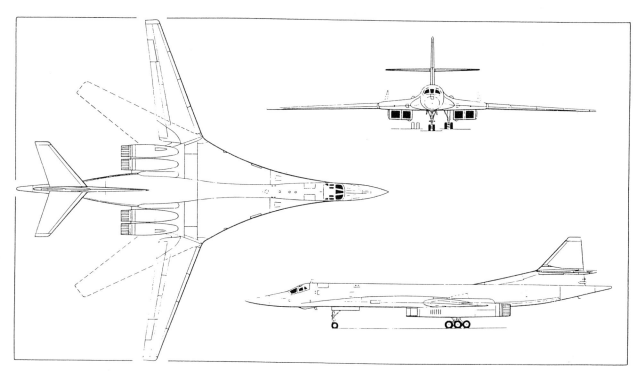

Helix

While the Mil bureau has had a monopoly of Soviet ground-based attack and assault helicopters, their ship equivalents have been the preserve of the Kamov bureau, presumably because of the latter's small-diameter contra-rotating rotors. In terms of large-scale produc-

tion, the Kamov series began with the 280 hp piston-engined Ka-15, which first flew in 1954 and was used for pilot training and liaison duties. The Ka-26 *Hoodlum* had two 325 hp piston engines, and first flew in 1965, but was mainly used for civil purposes. The bureau's third-generation ship-based helicopter was the Ka-25K *Hormone*, which entered service around 1967,

Rolling slowly out of the cargo hold of an Aeroflot An-124, Mil's latest Mi-28 *Havoc* attack helicopter takes on an almost mouse-like appearance, thanks to its radar nose and lack of rotor blades.

powered by two 1000 shp gas turbines. *Hormone A* carries a comprehensive ASW fit, and has a weapons bay for torpedoes and depth charges. *Hormone B* has a larger nose radome and is probably used for anti-ship surveillance and targeting (ASST). *Hormone C* is a utility and SAR version.

Kamov's fourth generation is represented by the Ka-29 *Helix B*, which is essentially a much more powerful derivative of the Ka-25K, with two 2200 shp Isotov TV3-117 engines (similar to those of the Mi-24 and Mi-28), and with close support armament provisions. It has a gross weight of 26,455 lb (12,000 kg) and a rotor diameter of 52.15 ft (15.9 m). With rotors folded, length is reduced to 39 ft (11.9 m). Width is 18.5 ft (5.65 m) with weapon pylons attached, reducing to 14.4 ft (3.8 m) with pylons folded. Height is 17.7 ft (5.4 m).

Cruising speed is 121 knots (225 km/hr), and maximum speed is 143 knots (265 km/hr). Practical ceiling is 16,400 ft (5000 m), and range is 270 nm (500 km).

The Ka-29 was designed to fulfil a Naval Aviation requirement for a day/night all-weather naval transport and attack helicopter. It first flew in 1977, making it a contemporary of the MiG-29 and Su-27. The Ka-29 can carry 16 paratroops or up to 10 injured, including four on stretchers. If pressed into the SAR role, it can carry up to 25 survivors. Maximum payload is 8820 lb (4000 kg).

The crew cabin of the Ka-29 is pressurized and protected by amour plate, and six of the eight fuel tanks contain plastic foam to prevent fuel-air mixture explosions. Permanent armament consists of a four-barrel 7.62 mm Gatling-type machine gun, flexibly mounted in the right-hand side of the nose. It is normally protected from sea spray by a nose panel, which is swung down on struts when the gun is to be fired.

External weapons can be mounted on four pylons supported by a tubular framework mounted on the fuselage sides. A publicity leaflet shows the Ka-29 carrying four 57 mm rocket pods, but when the aircraft made its Western debut at Hannover in 1990 (ILA-90) it was shown with two 20-round 80 mm rocket pods inboard and a total of eight AT-6 *Spiral* missiles outboard. The outer pylons can alternatively take gunpods. Pintle-mounted machine guns can be mounted in the doorways on either side. The leaflet makes no reference to the ventral weapons bay, though this is presumably retained. The Ka-29 has an inverted periscopic sight with laser ranger (similar to that of the Mi-24), and what appears to be an IR searchlight, possibly indicating the use of semi-active homing missiles.

The Kamov bureau head is Sergei Victorovich Mikheev, but chief designer for the Ka-29 was Vjacheslav G Krigin, with Veniamin A Kasjanikov as his deputy.

Havoc

The Mil Mi-28 *Havoc* made its public debut at Paris '89, before the first photograph had been published. It was represented by the third development aircraft (side number 032), which three months later was to appear at Helitech '89 at Redhill in southern England.

The general impression created was that the Mi-28 is the Soviet Union's response to the AH-64 Apache, with some improvements (eg, in front-line operability, and pilot's field of view), though the Soviet aircraft is clearly inferior in terms of development timescale and night/adverse weather capability. The Mi-28 employs the same engines as the Mi-24 *Hind*, and the new design clearly benefits from that experience, but the airframes have little in common. In essence, the Mi-24 is a flying armoured personnel carrier, but the Mi-28 will be a flying tank.

The Mi-28 was painted in old-fashioned camouflage of medium green and brown, somewhat reminiscent of British WW2 colours. The demonstrations were performed by Mil's CTP Gourgen R Karapetian and by Viktor Tchigankov at Le Bourget, and by Yuri Shapaev at Redhill.

Although its betters the 60°/sec turn rate required, the Mi-28 has an inferior turning performance to the AH-64. The Soviet aircraft was nonetheless thrown around at both airshows with great confidence. It did, however, take a remarkably long time from engine-start to lift-off, suggesting a slow warm-up, technical problems, or a long checklist.

It is difficult to establish with confidence who actually designed the Mi-28. The general designer of the Mil bureau is Marat Nikolaevich Tischenko, and his deputy is Mark Vladimirovich Vineberg. However, Alexei Ivanov has been reported to be the bureau's chief designer, and Andre Ermakov has often been mentioned in the Mi-28 context, possibly indicating that he is (or was) the project engineer in charge.

The first of three development aircraft (side number 012) had its maiden flight on 10 November 1982. In the course of test flying, it suffered a failure of the tail rotor drive shaft, following which the shaft material was changed from composites to aluminium alloy. This first aircraft was repaired and resumed development flying.

The second Mi-28 (022) was at least initially equipped (like the first) with a three-blade tail rotor, as in the case of the Mi-24. However, the third aircraft introduced a 12.6 ft (3.84 m) diameter 'flattened-X' tail rotor, similar to that of the AH-64. The Mi-28 has had its tail rotor on the right from the outset, whereas for practical purposes all Mi-24s have their tail rotors on the left. The Mi-24 has a horizontal tail surface on either side of the boom, but the Mi-28 has a single strut-braced surface on the left side of the fin. It may be noted that the first aircraft was exhibited at Tushino in '89, but at time of writing this second aircraft has never been shown.

The Mi-28's five main rotor blades are of composite honeycomb construction, with filament-wound spars, whereas the spars of the Mi-24 blades are made in titanium. The transmission system has also been redesigned, and the Mi-28 is reported to have electronic engine

Aircraft '032' was the third of three Mi-28 prototypes, the first making its initial flight on 10 November 1982. This close-up shows the armoured gunners' cockpit with the flexibly-mounted 30 mm cannon. (*Tony Holmes*)

control, with a flat rating to 10,000 ft (3000 m). At Paris-89 the development aircraft were said to have accumulated a total of 800 flight hours, representing around 90 per cent of the required total.

Aside from the early accident, development has suffered from delays with avionics and sensors, and there has been a weight-growth problem. Nonetheless, series production is expected to begin around 1991, and (despite the advanced nature of the aircraft) exports are planned, though probably with a different avionics fit to that supplied for home use.

Relative to the Mi-24, the deletion of the troop compartment has made possible a somewhat smaller and lighter airframe. Height has been reduced from 21.3 to 15.8 ft (6.5 to 4.8 m) to facilitate carriage in transport aircraft, though (unlike the AH-64 case) the main rotor blades cannot be folded and thus have to be removed. Possibly for the same reason, the span of the stub-wing has been reduced from 21.8 to 16.0 ft (6.65 to 4.874 m), although this also reduces the number of hardpoints from six to four.

The Mi-28 data-board at these shows gave a maximum weight of 25,137 lb (11,400 kg), though the leaflet information gives 22,930 lb (10,400 kg). Empty weight was reported from interviews as either 14,333 or 15,435 lb (6500 or 7000 kg). Full internal fuel was given as 3310 lb (1500 kg) by the pilot at Helitech, though the demonstrations were flown with only 2205 lb (1000 kg).

Whereas the engines of the Mi-24 are mounted side-by-side and ahead of the main rotor mast, these same Isotov (Leningrad bureau) TV3-117s are in the case of the Mi-28 located further aft, well separated on either side of the CG. The intakes are equipped with particle-separators, and on the aircraft exhibited (which was prob-

ably not representative of production standard) the exhausts were turned downwards and fitted with ducts to induce diluting air and thus reduce IR signature.

Maximum speed was given as 164.6 knots (305 km/hr), although the pilot at Helitech said 162 knots (300 km/hr), with full armament and fuel. Cruise speed is 143 knots (265 km/hr). The fact that the Mi-28 is slower than the Mi-24 is explained by the former's fixed (tailwheel) undercarriage and high-drag cannon installation. As in the case of the AH-64, a fixed tailwheel arrangement was probably adopted to save cost and weight (and reduce drag, relative to a fixed tricycle).

Maximum hover height is 11,800 ft (3600 m) OGE, and practical ceiling is 19,700 ft (6000 m), both significantly higher than for the heavier Mi-24. The range of the Mi-28 is given as 254 nm (470 km) and its endurance as two hours.

The stub-wing and external stores of the Mi-28 are directly abreast of the rotor mast, whereas those of the Mi-24 are set further aft. This appears to indicate that in the case of the older aircraft the clean CG is well forward (due to engine location)
and that external loads bring the CG aft to the rotor mast, whereas the Mi-28's CG position is virtually independent of take-off weight.

The two cockpits of the Mi-28 are naturally much narrower than those of the Mi-24 (which has a wide fuselage to accommodate an eight-man cabin). Compared to the Mi-24, the control functions involved in preparing for take-off are reportedly reduced from 120 to 10, though the Mi-28 certainly did not leap into the air at Redhill. Unlike the Mi-24, the new aircraft has no flying controls in the front cockpit.

The Mi-28's cockpit enclosures take the form of flat bulletproof panels of glass, significantly closer to the heads of the crew. This sounds claustrophobic, but the cockpit design was in fact widely admired, as giving an excellent field of view for an aircraft of this type. Both crew members sit in armoured surrounds, reported variously as titanium bathtubs or composite armour panels. The 50 mm windows are stated to be proof against 7.62 mm fire, and to provide some protection against 12 mm. The fuel tanks in

---

In discussing the Mi-28, it is difficult not to present a series of comparisons with the AH-64 Apache, but in terms of performance, the US helicopter has the edge, despite flying seven years earlier.
(*McDonnell Douglas Helicopter Company*)

Soviet experience in Afghanistan helped define the basic requirements for a rugged attack helicopter. Consequently, the Mi-28 is heavily protected against ground-fire and heat-seeking missiles.
(*Roy Braybrook*)

the lower centre fuselage are also protected with armour.

One unique feature of the Mi-28 is that provisions are being developed to allow the crew to bale out in the event of an emergency at altitude. When (or if) perfected, a single ring-pull will release both harnesses, jettison the pilot's door on the right and the gunner's on the left, release the stub-wings, and inflate bladders housed in fairings just below the cockpits. The crew will then take to the silk in the traditional (pre-ejection) way, with the inflated bladders throwing them clear of the mainwheels.

Continuing the survival theme, it is as a direct result of Soviet experience in Afghanistan that the Mi-28 has a small compartment in the centre fuselage, large enough to accommodate both crew members from a downed helicopter. In peacetime this space might be used occasionally to transport groundcrew. It is windowless, and emergency entry with the engines running would be an uncomfortable experience, since access (on the left side) means passing very close to the exhaust. It was noted after the Mi-28 had landed at Redhill, that the tarmac below the exhaust had begun to melt. However, in wartime some transient discomfort is clearly preferable to being taken prisoner.

The Mi-28 was exhibited with a total of 16 AT-6 *Spiral* tube-launched missiles on the wing-tips, two 20-round 80 mm rocket pods on the pylons, and a chin-mounted 30 mm cannon. This Model 2A42 gun is taken from the BMP-2 infantry fighting vehicle, and has a dual-feed system with a 130-round shell-box on eithr side, allowing the gunner to switch from (for example) high explosive to armour-piercing ammunition.

The cyclic rate is 300 rd/min for air-to-ground use, and 900 rd/min air-to-air.

The gun can be directed 13° above the horizontal, 40° below, and 110° on either side of the nose, controlled by the gunner's HMS. It has recently been reported that total azimuth travel has been increased from 220° to 240°, and that a new type of gun is under test on the first development aircraft. During the Le Bourget briefings it was admitted that a significant weight penalty had been accepted with the Model 2A42, in order to ensure the availability of suitable ammunition when operating from front-line sites. The report of a new gun suggests that on reflection this weight penalty may be considered to be excessive.

The Mi-28 is believed to have the same millimetre-wave AT-6 beam-riding guidance system as the Mi-24, but the antenna has been moved from an external pod to a thimble radome

on the nose. A daylight targeting turret with inverted periscopic sight and laser ranger is located directly below this radome. Unlike the Mi-24, there are no mechanical eyelids to protect this window, but it does have its own wiper. In the case of the third development Mi-28, slightly further aft and on either side of this turret were forward-looking window blanks, presumably where the FLIR and LLTV sensors will be fitted. On the subject of avionics, the Mi-28 employs Doppler radar navigation, and the flying controls system is stated to include hover- and heading-hold modes to facilitate armour engagements.

Projected developments include an analogue FBW system, and possibly pressurised cockpits for operations in an NBC environment. Six versions of the aircraft are planned, beginning with the anti-tank model (possibly equipped with a later missile, such as an airborne development of the AT-7 *Saxhorn*, or the AT-9). Other variants will include a dedicated air combat model, one for an unspecified 'anti-missile' role, and one to cover amphibious landings. This may indicate that the Mi-28 will compete with the Kamov *Hokum*, discussed later in this chapter.

More than any other helicopter, the Mi-28 was designed to fight and overnight with front-line

---

If they all work, eight *Spiral* (AT-6) anti-tank missiles, two rocket pods and the cannon would present a formidable response to an armoured attack. The Mi-28 itself would also present a smaller target than the bulky Mi-24 *Hind*.
(*Roy Braybrook*)

ground units. The effects of this design emphasis are to be seen in such features as the extremely low-pressure tyres, the use of army ammunition, and the ability to carry out basic servicing tasks using tools from ground vehicles. Its normal fuel is equivalent to JP-4, but in an all-out war the engines can be adjusted to operate for 24 hr on tank diesel fuel, although they would then be junked.

Comparing the Mi-24 with the AH-64, the Soviet product is running on a much later timescale, is somewhat larger and heavier, and is currently less advanced in terms of equipment for night/adverse weather operations. The

Apache first flew on 30 September 1975, more than seven years in advance of the Mi-28. Apache deliveries began in January 1984, and IOC was announced in July 1986, both dates suggesting that the gap has not diminished.

Rather than the Mi-28's two separate cockpits, the AH-64 has a single crew area, divided by a transparent blast shield above the pilot's instrument panel. The night sensors of the Mi-28 will evidently look straight forward through fixed windows, whereas the AH-64 has turret-mounted sensors with an azimuth travel of 180° for the pilot and 240° for the gunner's system.

The 30 mm Model 2A42 gun of the Mi-28 is said to be harder hitting than the 30 mm M230 Chain Gun of the AH-64, but the latter fires at 625 rd/min, compared to 300 rd/min (air-to-ground), and is fed from a remote magazine holding 320–1200 rounds, compared to only 240 for the Mi-28. The Mi-28's direct mounting of the shell boxes on the gun presumably gives a more reliable feed, but the sheer weight of the rotating

---

The Kamov Design Bureau has continued its flair in developing co-axial helicopters with the Ka-27/29/32 series. Known to NATO as *Helix*, the Ka-32 version is a civil derivative of the Ka-27, which in turn is a replacement for the Soviet Navy's shipborne fleet of Ka-25s (NATO name *Hormone*).

mass implies a heavy mounting and may well restrict angular acceleration as it slews round to bear on the target.

Comparing unguided rocket projectiles, the new Soviet 80 mm may well be superior to the American 2.75-inch (70 mm) FFAR. On the other hand, the tube-launched, beam-riding AT-6 appears to be a very small-calibre missile, and is probably inferior in accuracy and hitting power to the laser-homing Rockwell Hellfire of the AH-64. The balance, may, however, be redressed by one of the later Soviet anti-tank missiles known to exist.

Compared to the 2200 shp Isotov engines of the Mi-28, the T700-GE-701s of the AH-64 are rated at 1696 shp for normal operations, and thus give 23 per cent less power at sea level. The maximum attack mission weight of the AH-64 is 17,640 lb (8000 kg), which is 23 per cent less than the 22,930 lb (10,400 kg) published for the Mi-28.

The AH-64's internal fuel of 2550 lb (1156 kg) is 23 per cent less than that for the Mi-28. Range on internal fuel is 260 m (480 km) for the AH-64, which is virtually identical to the Mi-28 figure.

Attracting comparatively little coverage in the technical aviation Press at the 1990 Hannover Show was the Ka-29, yet this compact assault helicopter is likely to be around for many years to come and will equip a number of the Soviet Navy's carriers and assault ships.
(*Roy Braybrook*)

However, the AH-64 also has a ferry range of 800 nm (1480 km) with four 183 Imp gal (835 litre) tanks. It is doubtful whether the Mi-28 has provisions for external fuel.

Most performance figures for the two helicopters are very similar. The AH-64's maximum level speed of 160 knots (196 km/hr) is marginally inferior, but its cruise speed of 147–155 knots (272–287 km/hr) is slightly better than that for the Mi-28. Likewise, the AH-64's 11,500 ft (3500 m) OGE hover ceiling is slightly inferior, but its service ceiling of 21,000 ft (6400 m) is slightly better.

To summarize, the Mi-28 is somewhat larger and heavier than the Apache, and may thus be expected to have a better warload-radius performance. It is also better equipped to live with front-line ground forces. By the time it is in large-scale service in the mid-1990s, it may be armed with very advanced anti-tank missiles, though one may suspect that its avionics fit will lag behind that of the McDonnell Douglas aircraft.

Hokum

In mid-1984 Western intelligence became aware that the Soviet Union had begun test flying a high performance helicopter with contra-rotating rotors in the Kamov tradition. This aircraft was subsequently designated *Hokum* by NATO. The general impression created by the various Pentagon leaks during the 1980s was that *Hokum* was to be a dedicated attack helicopter, and a possible alternative to *Havoc*.

In May 1989, Kamov's deputy designer-general Alexseievich Kasjenikov (interviewed at a meeting of the American Helicopter Society in Boston) denied that the bureau was developing a 'Ka-41 *Hokum*' attack helicopter, a denial that was repeated by Kamov representatives at Redhill four months later. One possible explanation for such denials is that the rumoured Ka-41 designation is incorrect, and that Kamov interprets the term 'attack helicopter' in purely a land-based sense. In any event, the Pentagon's *SMP-89*, published in September 1989, included a reasonably good surface-to-air photograph of *Hokum*, thus eliminating any suspicion that the

programme had been terminated, or that US intelligence had imagined the whole thing.

In essence, *Hokum* is a high-speed naval attack compound helicopter that is currently under flight test, and is presumably intended to provide Soviet Naval Infantry with close air support, and air defence against hostile helicopters.

It has two three-blade contra-rotating rotors, side-by-side seating, a large-span wing with endplates, and a single vertical tail supplemented by small fins on the tips of the fuselage-mounted tailplane. It seems likely that the seating arrangement and the location of the tailplane were both chosen to restrict hangar space demands, the former producing a shorter front fuselage and the latter facilitating a fuselage articulation just aft of the tailplane. Kamov rotors fold routinely, and the wing may be assumed to fold for the same reason.

The important point about the design of *Hokum* is that the remarkable span of the wing indicates that it plays a major role in supporting the helicopter's weight in forward flight, thus offloading the rotors and making unusually high speeds possible. It is noteworthy that *Hokum* appears to have conventional (fixed-wing type) rudder, ailerons and trailing edge flap surfaces.

In the *SMP-89* document, *Hokum* is illustrated as a relatively small helicopter, with a fuselage only about 50 ft (15 m) long, It is nonetheless possible that it is equipped with the same 2200 shp engines as the Mi-28, using the power to attain high forward speeds, rather than to take off at a high weight. The Pentagon prediction of a maximum speed of 190 knots (350 km/hr) could be an underestimate. To put this estimate into perspective, the current helicopter speed record was established by a Westland Lynx in 1986 at 216.45 knots (400.87 km/hr).

Toward A New Generation

In early 1988 America's DNI, Rear Adm William O Studeman, referred to the Soviets developing a second-generation V/STOL fighter/attack aircraft, designated Yak-41. In *SMP-89* an artist's impression appeared of this aircraft on the deck of a *Tbilisi*-class carrier, alongside the subsonic

Yak-38 from which it is conceptually derived.

If the Pentagon drawing is accurate, then the Yak-41 retains what may be termed a 'twin-lift plus lift/cruise' powerplant configuration, but the latter engine and associated intakes are revised for supersonic performance. The switch to two Vigilante-style multi-shock intakes leads to the use of two vertical tails. Strangely, these are mounted at either lateral extremity of a beavertail rear fuselage. This suggests that, rather than having two thrust-vectoring nozzles (like the Yak-38), a single nozzle is used for compatibility with an afterburner.

It may be recalled that in the context of German V/STOL strike-fighter studies in the 1960s, British and US engine manufacturers proposed various forms of bending reheat pipes. More recently, Rolls-Royce has proposed to achieve the same effect by turning jetpipe segments about two 45° skewed planes. It will thus be interesting to see how the Soviets have produced thrust-vectoring with an afterburning engine.

Whether the Soviets would really operate a relatively small V/STOL aircraft, with all this implies in terms of performance penalties, from the *Tbilisi* (and the subsequent *Varyag* and the larger 75,000 ton *Ulyanovsk*), alongside the much more capable Su-27 air superiority fighter, the multi-role MiG-29, and the Su-25 close support aircraft, may be open to doubt. It seems more likely that the Yak-41 would be restricted to the *Kiev* class, which can take only V/STOL aeroplanes and helicopters.

In Conclusion

If the Soviets had maintained their momentum in the field of combat aircraft, then one would have expected the first prototypes of a fifth generation of postwar fighters to have begun flying in the second half of the 1980s. The impression created by leaks from US intelligence services is, however, that the Yak-41 is the only significant new combat aircraft to have begun flight trials in the Soviet Union during this period. The fact that this may become the world's first production supersonic V/STOL aircraft makes it interesting

in both a technical and a historic sense, but the Yak-41 hardly has the military significance of the Su-27, or even the MiG-29. One might add that Britain could easily have produced a better supersonic V/STOL aircraft in the 1960s.

In terms of conventional fighters, recent issues of the Pentagon's *SMP* publication have indicated that the Soviets are 'probably' developing new air combat fighters, but this assessment has not been backed by photographic evidence. This apparent absence of a new generation is strange, in view of the well-published West European philosophy that an unstable delta-canard configuration will provide significant improvements in supersonic manoeuvrability. In the West, this concept was first tested with the unmanned Rockwell HiMAT test vehicle, which flew on 27 July 1989. This was followed by Dassault's Rafale A, which flew on 4 July 1986, and BAe's EAP, which flew on 8 August 1986. The same sort of configuration will be employed by the four-nation Eurofighter EFA. This may be regarded as a derivative of MBB's TKF-90, which was exhibited as a full-scale mockup at Hannover in 1980.

If the current Western perception is correct, and there is as yet no fifth postwar Soviet combat aircraft generation flying, then this may be explained by a combination of factors. Firstly, the fourth generation (notably the Su-27) has been so delayed that the urgency for a new generation has not yet arisen. Secondly, defence funding restrictions and the thaw in East-West relations also militate in favour of delaying any major new development programme. Thirdly, the Soviets may have tested the delta-canard configuration in their wind tunnels, and concluded that it has little real advantage over the Su-27 development with foreplanes. Fourthly, the Soviets may well have waited to see the YF-22 and -23 stealth fighters before committing to a new fighter programme. Having made all these points, the absence of a technology demonstrator programme is still surprising.

Finally, it must be emphasized that we may know everything the Soviets are flying, but we certainly do not know what they have in the wind tunnels at TsAGI. Judging by the quality of the Su-27 and MiG-29, perhaps we in the West can sleep better, not knowing.

Abbreviations

AAA	anti-aircraft artillery	EFA	European Fighter Aircraft
AAM	air-to-air missile	ELINT	electronic intelligence
AC	aerodynamic centre		
ADC	air data computer	FBW	fly-by-wire
AEW	airborne early warning	FMS	Foreign Military Sales
ALCM	air-launched cruise missile	FOD	foreign object damage
AOA	angle of attack		
APU	auxiliary power unit	GD	General Dynamics
ASCC	Air Standard Coordinating Committee	GE	General Electric
		GGS	gyro gunsight
ASI	airspeed indicator		
ASW	anti-submarine warfare	HiMAT	Highly Maneuverable Aircraft Technology
ATE	automatic test equipment		
ATGW	anti-tank guided weapon	HMS	helmet-mounted sight
		HUD	head-up display
BAC	British Aircraft Corporation		
BAe	British Aerospace	IAS	indicated airspeed
		IDS	InterDiction/Strike
CAF	Canadian Armed Forces	IOC	initial operational capability
CAP	combat air patrol	IRST	infrared search-and-track
CAS	chief of air staff		
CATIC	China Export-Import Corporation	JATO	jet-assisted take-off
CG	centre of gravity		
		LEX	leading edge extension
COCOM	COordinating COMmittee for multi-lateral export controls		
		MAD	magnetic anomaly detector
COIN	counter-insurgency	MoD	Ministry of Defence
CRT	cathode-ray tube	MoU	memorandum of understanding
CTOL	conventional take-off and landing	MTBF	mean time between failures
CTP	chief test pilot		
		NBC	nuclear, bacteriological and chemical
DNI	director of naval intelligence	NF	night fighter
DOSAAF	Voluntary Association for Assistance for the Armed Services	NORAD	North American Air Defense
		NVNAF	North Vietnam Air Force
DWP	Defence White Paper		
		OKB	experimental design bureau
EAP	Experimental Aircraft Programme	OR	operational requirement

PLAAF	People's Liberation Army Air Force	STOL	short take-off and landing
RAAF	Royal Australian Air Force	TAS	true airspeed
RAE	Royal Aerospace Establishment	TBO	time between overhauls
R-R	Rolls-Royce	TsAGI	Central Fluid Dynamics Institute
RWR	radar-warning receiver	TsIAM	Central Aero-Engine Institute
SAF	Soviet Air Force	VLF	very low frequency
SAM	surface-to-air missile	V/STOL	vertical or short take-off and landing
SFC	specific fuel consumption	VTOL	vertical take-off and landing
SMP	*Soviet Military Power*		
SRAM	Short-Range Attack Missile	WPAFB	Wright-Patterson Air Force Base
SST	supersonic transport	WW	World War

Index

Bell X-1 **41**
  X-5 **105**
  X-14 **130, 131**

Chengdu F-7/J-7 **81–84**
Convair B-58 **102**

Domodedovov **8, 28, 103**

GD F-111 **105**
Grumman F-14 **105**
Guizhou FT-7 **20**

Harbin H-6/B-6 **56**
Hawker P.1127 **105**

Ilyushin Il-2 **19**
  Il-10 **19**
  Il-22 **50**
  Il-28 **51–52**
  Il-54 **102**

Kamov Ka-15 **190**
  Ka-26 **190**
  Ka-25K **190**
  Ka-29 **190**
  'Ka-41' **200**
Korean War **39**

Lavochkin La-15 **26**
  La-152 **35**
  La-160 **35, 36**
  La-176 **40**
  La-190 **43**

Myasischev M-4 **27, 58**
  M-50 **101**
Mil Mi-17 **139**
  Mi-24/25/35 **28, 138–145**
  Mi-28 **28, 191–200**
Mikoyan OKB **9**
  MiG-9 **33**
  MiG-15 **10, 11, 37–40**
  MiG-17 **14, 26, 41–43**
  MiG-19 **12, 26, 44–47**
  MiG-21 **12, 20, 70–84**
  MiG-23/27 **20, 106–117**
  MiG-25 **12, 92–96**
  MiG-31 **153–156**
  Ye-152A **84**
  Ye-166A **24, 84**
  Ye-230 **25**
  Ye-231 **24, 105**
  Ye-266 **95**

Nanchang A-5/Q-5 **47, 48**

Panavia Tornado **105**

Rockwell B-1 **186**

Shorts SC.1 **105**
Shenyang J-8/F-8 **86, 87**
Simonov **28, 170**
Sukhoi OKB **66**
  Su-7 **22, 70**
  Su-9 **87**
  Su-10 **51**
  Su-11 **88**

Su-15 **25, 28, 91**
Su-17 **12, 118–121**
Su-24 **12, 28, 121–126**
Su-25 **12, 15, 16, 19, 26, 28, 145–152**
Su-27 **10, 12, 15, 28, 169–186**
Su-100 **170**

Tbilisi-class **201**
Tischenko **412**
TsAGI **22, 157**
Tupolev Tu-4 **50**
  Tu-16 **27, 52–57**
  Tu-22 **28, 97–102**
  Tu-22M **28, 127–130**
  Tu-28P **90**
  Tu-95/142 **58–63**
  Tu-98 **102**
  Tu-160 **28, 186–189**
Tushino **9**

Yakovlev Yak-15 **32**
  Yak-17 **35**
  Yak-23 **36**
  Yak-25 **27, 50**
  Yak-28 **28, 89, 96**
  Yak-30 **41**
  Yak-36 **25, 130, 131**
  Yak-38 **26, 28, 132–137**
  Yak-41 **28, 200, 201**
  Yak-1000 **44**